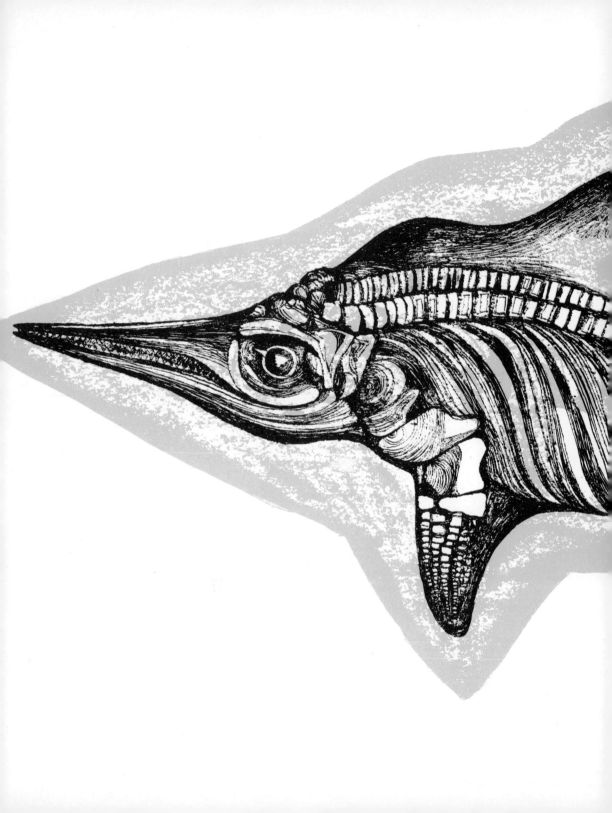

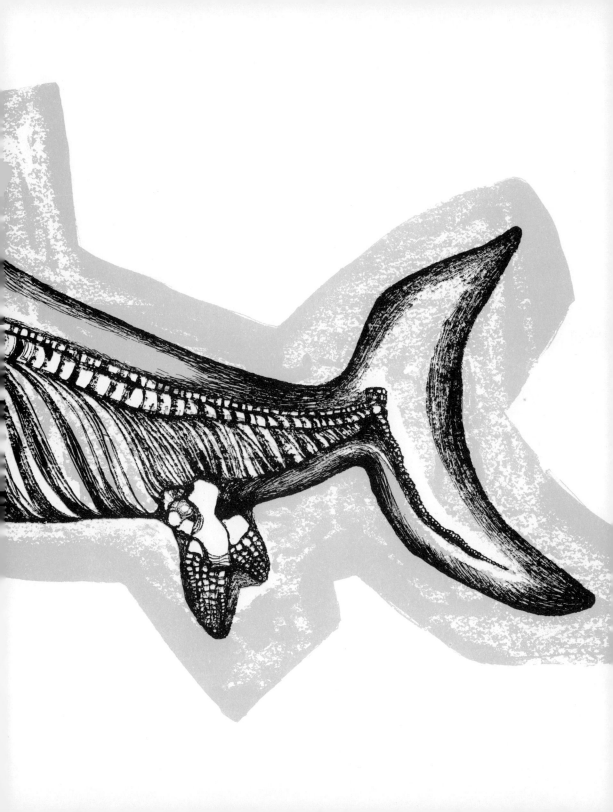

QUEST FOR PREHISTORY

This book is written for children who are excited by the romance of archaeology and who want to know something of the background to the great discoveries and to understand the pattern of life as it unfolded from the first stirrings in the shallow seas to the appearance of human beings; and from the first stone tool makers to the skilled workers in bronze and iron at the end of prehistoric times. Reptiles and mammals, apes and near-men, Old and New Stone Age men, Beaker Folk and Belgae — we meet them all.

The plot of this fascinating mystery story is outlined simply and concisely; and the way in which the clues that help to make the puzzle clearer were discovered by archaeologists — the detectives of history — is described with compelling clarity. Archaeology is shown as a science, an art, and an adventure. The part that children have played in some of the most thrilling discoveries is highlighted in order to stimulate the young reader's enthusiasm, and to create a desire to share in the search for the secrets of the past that the earth still holds.

QUEST
FOR PREHISTORY

by
GEOFREY PALMER
and
NOEL LLOYD

with illustrations by
CAROL BARKER

THE JOHN DAY COMPANY   **NEW YORK**

TO
Margaret Clayton
and
Colin Lloyd

FIRST AMERICAN EDITION 1966

*Text Copyright © 1965 by Geoffrey Palmer and Noel
Lloyd. Illustrations Copyright © 1965 by Dobson Books, Ltd.
All rights reserved. No part of this book may be reprinted,
or reproduced in any form or by any means electronic,
mechanical or other (including but not limited to photo-
copying, recording, or a process of information storage and
retrieval), without permission in writing from the Pub-
lisher, The John Day Company, Inc., 62 West 45th Street,
New York, N.Y. 10036.*

Library of Congress Catalogue Card Number: 66-10845

PRINTED IN THE UNITED STATES OF AMERICA

CONTENTS

Chapter One

THE WORLD BEGINS

WE ARE GOING to start our quest for prehistory at the very beginning of the world, long before there were any animals or human beings living on the earth, and it will take us from the vast empty planet whirling around in space up to the time when written history begins.

We will meet all sorts of strange creatures in our journey through the far distant past, and we will discover how our knowledge of what happened millions of years ago has been put together bit by bit, like a jigsaw puzzle or a detective story.

Our detectives, however, do not set out to capture robbers or murderers. They are looking for the past, trying to find out what the world was like when it first began; how it became as it is today; what sort of creatures the first animals were; when man first came on the scene, and how he changed from a hairy, apelike creature to a skilled hunter and artist. A scientist examines a piece of rock, a shell, a fragment of bone, a piece of broken pot or a flint tool, and from such things he can build up a picture of life as it was thousands and even millions of years ago — just as a detective can tell from a footprint that it was made by a tall man weighing 154 pounds who walks with a limp.

The important words with which we start our quest are

paleontology, *prehistory* and *archaeology*. Paleontology is the study of extinct animals and plants and is concerned with the time before there were any men in the world. Prehistory is the story of man before there were any written records to tell us what had been happening. Archaeology, which also embraces prehistory, is the study of the relics that man has left behind him and the story they tell of his life and times. It makes no distinction between the times before and after writing was invented.

Thus the paleontologist, the prehistorian and the archaeologist are all the detectives of history. The clues they seek are bones, pottery, tools, weapons and ornaments that are found in rocks, in ruined and buried cities, in caves, quarries, graves and tombs. Artifacts, the things that men make with their hands, are the special interest of the prehistorian, for they often tell more of the truth about early man than anything that could have been written down. Objects made of wood, leather or cloth rot away very easily, but tools and weapons of stone, bone or metal, and the fossilized remains of men and animals, do not.

The archaeologist looks for these things, too, and also for the clay tablets and cylinders, the monuments and papyri on which scribes have recorded the history of their times.

12

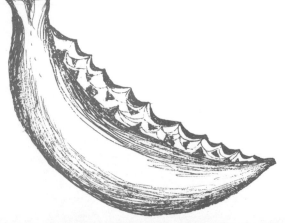

The paleontologist helps to build up the picture of the life of past ages by studying the fossils found in rocks. He looks for the footprints, the bones and fossilized remains of extinct plants, animals and other creatures, and not only does he discover things about the owners of the footprints and the bones, but also about the age of the rocks in which they are found.

The quest involves hard labor, patience and determination. Our detectives may excavate for months and find nothing. On the other hand, they may come across exciting and valuable evidence on their first day of work. Sometimes they have to dig deep into the ruins of an ancient city, burrow in underground caves or dredge the bed of a river — or they might stub their toes against a pot of coins in a field turned up by the plow or pick up a piece of flint shaped into an arrowhead in a gravel pit.

But there is romance in archaeology as well as hard work. Heinrich Schliemann, for instance, was determined even as a boy that one day he would find the ruins of the city of Troy, and when he was grown up this came true. Many beautiful and valuable objects have been found by accident, and children have made important archaeological finds such as the wonderful cave paintings done thousands of years ago which were discovered by some French boys looking for a lost dog.

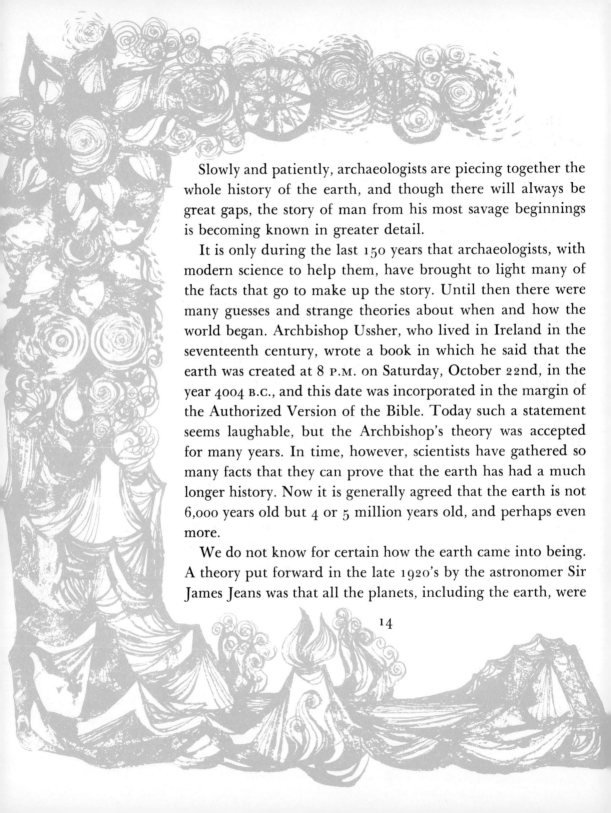

Slowly and patiently, archaeologists are piecing together the whole history of the earth, and though there will always be great gaps, the story of man from his most savage beginnings is becoming known in greater detail.

It is only during the last 150 years that archaeologists, with modern science to help them, have brought to light many of the facts that go to make up the story. Until then there were many guesses and strange theories about when and how the world began. Archbishop Ussher, who lived in Ireland in the seventeenth century, wrote a book in which he said that the earth was created at 8 P.M. on Saturday, October 22nd, in the year 4004 B.C., and this date was incorporated in the margin of the Authorized Version of the Bible. Today such a statement seems laughable, but the Archbishop's theory was accepted for many years. In time, however, scientists have gathered so many facts that they can prove that the earth has had a much longer history. Now it is generally agreed that the earth is not 6,000 years old but 4 or 5 million years old, and perhaps even more.

We do not know for certain how the earth came into being. A theory put forward in the late 1920's by the astronomer Sir James Jeans was that all the planets, including the earth, were

14

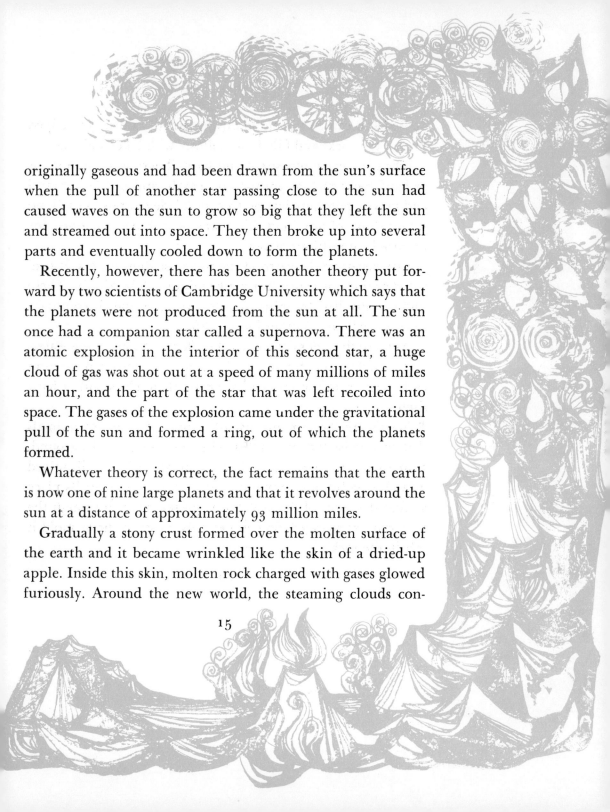

originally gaseous and had been drawn from the sun's surface when the pull of another star passing close to the sun had caused waves on the sun to grow so big that they left the sun and streamed out into space. They then broke up into several parts and eventually cooled down to form the planets.

Recently, however, there has been another theory put forward by two scientists of Cambridge University which says that the planets were not produced from the sun at all. The sun once had a companion star called a supernova. There was an atomic explosion in the interior of this second star, a huge cloud of gas was shot out at a speed of many millions of miles an hour, and the part of the star that was left recoiled into space. The gases of the explosion came under the gravitational pull of the sun and formed a ring, out of which the planets formed.

Whatever theory is correct, the fact remains that the earth is now one of nine large planets and that it revolves around the sun at a distance of approximately 93 million miles.

Gradually a stony crust formed over the molten surface of the earth and it became wrinkled like the skin of a dried-up apple. Inside this skin, molten rock charged with gases glowed furiously. Around the new world, the steaming clouds con-

densed and caused torrential downpours of rain which helped to cool the rocks and filled the hollows with lakes and seas.

Then the earth was silent and bare. There were mountains of hard rocks such as granite and basalt, and beaches of sand and gravel, but there was no tree, no blade of grass, no soil, no living thing of any kind. This was how things remained for hundreds of millions of years.

Life began on the earth in the warm, shallow waters. It consisted of tiny one-celled things like minute blobs of jelly. These blobs multiplied by splitting into two, each half becoming a separate cell and another blob of life.

As these tiny cells developed they floated about in the water, soft, boneless and blind, but in time they absorbed calcium carbonate from the water and coated themselves with a hard shell.

Fossils are the remains, usually stony, of plants or animals that have resisted decay and have become buried in the ground. Sometimes the hard part of the animal will have dissolved away bit by bit, and mineral matter will have taken its place so that the form of the skeleton is preserved even though the material has changed. Sometimes only a cast, print or mold is left in the rock.

16

Herodotus, a Greek traveler and historian born in the fifth century B.C. and called the Father of History, was one of the first men to guess what fossils really are. He traveled widely in western Greece, Asia Minor, Syria, Egypt and Mesopotamia, studying the customs and history of the people. When he was in the desert, he saw some fossils which had at one time been living sea creatures, and this led him to think that the Mediterranean Sea had once spread over North Africa, and that when it retreated the fossils had been left behind.

One interesting example of a fossil is a prehistoric fly caught and preserved in amber, the fossilized gum from extinct pine trees. Many great animals of the past were caught in peat bogs or quicksand, and the skeletons of a hundred mastodons have been found in the peat bogs of Kentucky. Trees and plants in fossil form are not as common as animals, because they do not have a bony skeleton, but the imprints of leaves are sometimes found in coal, and there are forests of trees which have been turned to stone.

The paleontologist extracts his clues from the rocks with hammer and chisel, grinders and dentist's drills. Buried pots and tools tell the story of what happened thousands of years

17

ago, but fossils speak of a time, millions of years ago, when the earth was inhabited by strange and alarming creatures.

How do archaeologists *know* how old things are? At one time they had to guess the age of an old object, but today dating is more accurate, though it is a complicated scientific problem. There are several methods. The most reliable way of assessing the relative age of a period comes from understanding the information collected about the tools, made by different groups. of early men, which are found in layers — the oldest at the bottom — and by studying the different types of implements made of flint, antler and bone. The distribution of relics in various parts of the world is also important because the migration of peoples, their colonies and trade routes, all help to fill in the picture.

Geochronology, which is the study of time scales in years which extend back into the very remote past, enters the archaeologist's work in three ways. One of them is studying the yearly growth rings seen on a section of tree trunk. Another involves examination of such things as bands or varves of silt and clay which were left each year by retreating ice sheets in the Ice Age. The third way is by the Radioactive Carbon, or Carbon 14, method, which was devised in 1946 by Professor Willard F. Libby, at that time head of a team of research workers at the

18

University of Chicago. He was awarded a Nobel Prize in chemistry in 1960.

Radioactive carbon comes from outer space and is absorbed by all living plants and animals. After they die, the radioactivity created by the carbon decays at a steady rate. In approximately 5,700 years it has been reduced by a half. When the remaining radioactive carbon in anything which has once lived is measured by a Geiger counter, it is possible to find out fairly accurately how long ago it died. This method involves burning the material that is being used, so it is only employed when there is material to spare.

Another aid to dating is by measuring the fluorine in bones. Fluorine is a substance found in soil, and is absorbed by buried bones. The longer bones have been buried, therefore, the more fluorine they will contain. Bones also contain nitrogen but when they are buried they gradually lose it. As they take in fluorine while losing the nitrogen, it is plain that the age of a bone can be calculated by the amounts of these two substances it contains; the more fluorine and the less nitrogen it has, the older it will be.

The age of rocks can be found by uranium dating. Disturbances caused by eruptions inside the earth sometimes result in pockets of hard igneous rocks, formed by volcanic action, being

forced up into layers of sedimentary rocks, which are those we can see in layers in quarries and the sides of mountains, and were formed by sediment being laid down on the beds of seas and lakes. The igneous rock may contain a radioactive metal called uranium. Uranium splits up and forms the gas helium and a kind of lead. When the amount of uranium which is left and the lead which has formed are both measured in one of these pockets of igneous rock, then the age of the sedimentary rock can be worked out.

A still newer method of rock dating has been devised recently at the University of California by Dr. J. F. Evenden and G. H. Curtis. It is similar to the Carbon 14 method, but is based on the fact that many rocks contain a small quantity of radioactive potassium. This decays more slowly than Carbon 14 and turns into argon, an inactive gaseous part of the atmosphere. The length of time since a volcanic rock has been formed can be calculated by measuring the amount of radioactive potassium against the amount of argon, and this method can give results over a much greater span of years than the Carbon 14 method.

Tests made on rock in which a skull was found in 1959 in the Olduvai Gorge, Tanganyika — and thought to be about

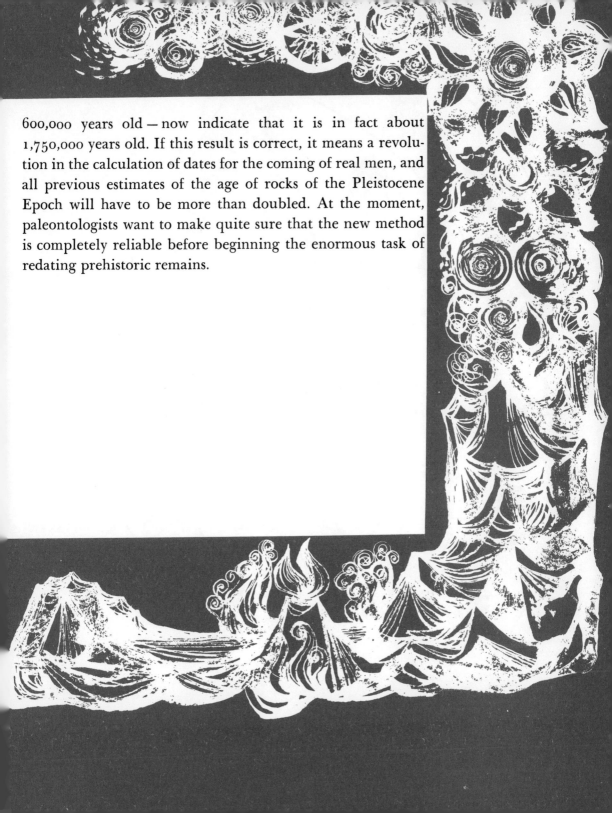

600,000 years old — now indicate that it is in fact about 1,750,000 years old. If this result is correct, it means a revolution in the calculation of dates for the coming of real men, and all previous estimates of the age of rocks of the Pleistocene Epoch will have to be more than doubled. At the moment, paleontologists want to make quite sure that the new method is completely reliable before beginning the enormous task of redating prehistoric remains.

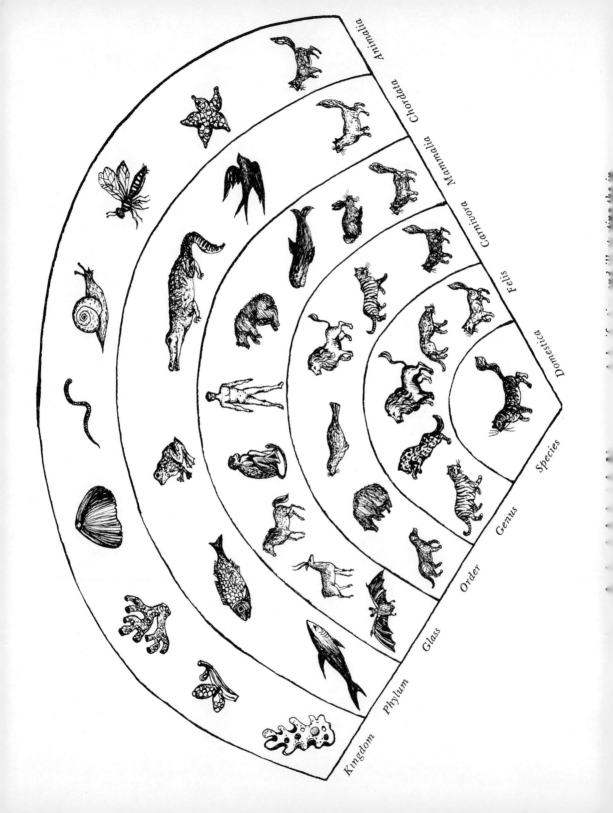

Kingdom · Phylum · Class · Order · Genus · Species

Animalia · Chordata · Mammalia · Carnivora · Felis · Domestica

Chapter Two

FIRST LIFE

FIVE THOUSAND MILLION years is such a vast length of time that it is beyond the bounds of our imagination. We will be able to understand better what has been happening during that time if we make a kind of calendar of Earth History. We will divide the calendar first into eras, and the eras into periods. An era is simply a length of time.

The earliest eras are the Azoic and the Proterozoic. Zoic is a Greek word meaning life; Azoic means without life; and Proterozoic means first life. These two eras cover the time from the beginning of the earth until about 600 million years ago. We already know that the earth was first of all in a molten state, and that the rocks formed were too hot to support any kind of life. But when the earth cooled, the first forms of life began to stir in the seas.

Next came the Paleozoic Era, the era of ancient life. It lasted for over 300 million years and definite fossils are found in Paleozoic rocks.

This was followed by the Mesozoic Era, the era of middle life, and it lasted for another 150 million years. It is often called the Age of Reptiles because these creatures were the lords of the earth.

The era in which we are living today began about 70 million years ago. It is the Cenozoic Era, the era of recent life. It is also the Age of Mammals, and it was during the latter part of this era that man appeared on the scene.

The names of the periods into which the eras are split are based on the kinds of rocks which were formed at certain times. Fossil records of the pre-Cambrian, which ended about 600 million years ago, include traces of tiny objects that may have been a kind of bacteria, algae, sponges or corals.

The Paleozoic Era is divided into six periods. The earliest is the Cambrian Period which lasted about a 100 million years. Cambria is the old Roman name for Wales, and it was in Wales that rocks of this period were first investigated. There was still no life on the land, but in the sea there were some highly developed creatures. One of them was the trilobite. More than a thousand different kinds of trilobites have been found in the Cambrian rocks, some only as big as a pin's head, others 18 inches long. This creature had a hard outer covering divided into three parts, long feelers, big eyes, and legs for walking. It lived in shallow water and ate seaweed and creatures smaller than itself.

24

There were many other invertebrates, or animals without a backbone, in the Cambrian seas. There were jellyfish, sponges and cephalopods. The latter were the ancestors of the octopus, cuttlefish and squid. There were brachiopods, too. Their popular name is Lamp Shell, because later varieties resembled a Roman lamp.

The second period of the Paleozoic Era is the Ordovician, and it covered the next 60 million years. It was named after rocks where a Celtic tribe called the Ordovices used to live. The only living things were still sea creatures, mollusks with soft bodies and hard outer shells.

Another Celtic tribe, the Silures, gave its name to the Silurian Period, which occupied the next 40 million years. The first fossil fishes are found in the rocks laid down in the last part of this period, though a strange kind of "fish," with no jaw, and covered with bony armor, lived in the late Ordovician Period.

The fourth period of the Paleozoic Era is the Devonian Period, so called because rocks of this period were found in Devon. It lasted for over 50 million years. Fish were now common, living in freshwater lakes, streams and seas. They had

simple lungs, and later in this period their fins changed to legs. They were the ancestors of frogs, toads and newts, which are amphibians. (An amphibian is cold-blooded, has a backbone and lungs, and limbs that can be used on land. The young amphibian usually lives in water and breathes through gills.)

Next came the Carboniferous Period, or Coal Age, and it lasted for 80 million years. This was a time of great swampy forests of huge ferns and trees, amphibians and giant insects. The story of coal began at this time. When the forests died others took their place. Land sank, forests drowned. The land rose again and more forests grew. This happened many times until there was layer upon layer of half-rotted vegetation at the bottom of the water. Finally the swamps became dry land. The layers were squeezed into the black material we call coal, and the mud in between the layers became the slaty rock called shale. The change from tree to coal took roughly 100,000 years, and seams of coal were being formed all through the Carboniferous Period.

The sixth and last period of the Paleozoic Era is the Permian Period, named after the old province of Perm in Russia where these rocks were first studied, and it lasted for 45 million years. The swampy coal forests had dwindled, and amphibians had to change so that they could live on land. The commonest land creature was the reptile. A reptile is a vertebrate, a creature with a backbone, and although it can live in water it can also live completely on land. The young of reptiles are usually produced in eggs with shells, and they hatch without gills. Their bodies are generally protected by layers of scales. The largest reptiles of the Permian Period were about 10 feet long. Some of them lived on plants, others on flesh.

Now we have arrived at the Mesozoic Era, which is divided into three periods. The first, which lasted about 45 million years, was the Triassic Period. Its name was given to it by mistake. *Trias* is a Greek word meaning three, and a German geologist of the nineteenth century named Freidrich von Alberti, who discovered that in Germany the layers of rock of this period could be divided into three main types, thought that this was so everywhere. He was wrong, but the name for this period remained. During the Triassic Period there was a great change in living creatures. There were still amphibians, but they already were giving way to reptiles. The first dinosaurs appeared. The word dinosaur means Terrible Lizard, and is applied to two groups of reptiles that lived during the Mesozoic Era. There were so many of them and they were so strange that they must have a chapter to themselves.

The Jurassic Period followed the Triassic and covered the

next 45 million years. It gets its name from the Jura Mountains in France, which were formed during that time. Dinosaurs became giants, slow moving and plant eating, and not nearly as terrifying as they looked. Flying and swimming reptiles were common and birds developed.

The next 65 million years saw the Cretaceous Period or Chalk Age. This is the period when chalk was formed, when reptilian life reached its peak and then was almost totally destroyed. It has been called the Time of the Great Dying. No one knows what really happened, but it was as though life had got out of hand, and a clean sweep had to be made so that the next stage of development could begin without the giant reptiles. Vast numbers of animals of all kinds simply disappeared and became extinct, both on land and in the sea. The chief creatures that seem to have lived on through this great destruction were crocodiles, turtles, birds and mammals. But before we follow them into the next era, we must retrace our steps and take a closer look at the Terrible Lizards, the dinosaurs.

Chapter Three

THE AGE OF REPTILES

THE FOSSILIZED REMAINS and footprints of dinosaurs found in rocks show that there were more than 5,000 kinds, from small to gigantic. Most of them lived on vegetation but a few were flesh-eaters. In spite of their size they had very small brains.

Perhaps the best known dinosaur is Brontosaurus, or Thunder Lizard. It was about 70 feet long and weighed 40 tons — or more than ten elephants! It had a small head, a very long neck and a huge tail. As its brain weighed less than a pound, it must have been a very stupid creature. Because of its small mouth and enormous size, it spent all its time eating, and had to wade about in shallow, swampy places and lift its neck up to the plants that formed its diet. Such a sluggish creature had no way of defending itself, so it kept to the water to avoid the fierce land dinosaurs.

Its cousin was Diplodocus, longer than Brontosaurus, because it had a tail like a whip, but not as heavy. Diplodocus had nostrils on top of its head so that it could breathe while the rest of its body was under water. It was gentle and harmless and lived only on plants.

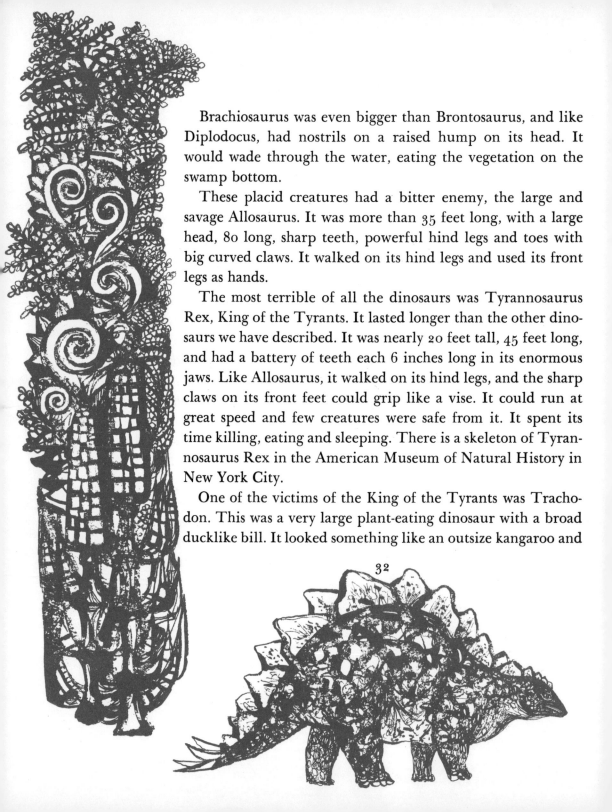

Brachiosaurus was even bigger than Brontosaurus, and like Diplodocus, had nostrils on a raised hump on its head. It would wade through the water, eating the vegetation on the swamp bottom.

These placid creatures had a bitter enemy, the large and savage Allosaurus. It was more than 35 feet long, with a large head, 80 long, sharp teeth, powerful hind legs and toes with big curved claws. It walked on its hind legs and used its front legs as hands.

The most terrible of all the dinosaurs was Tyrannosaurus Rex, King of the Tyrants. It lasted longer than the other dinosaurs we have described. It was nearly 20 feet tall, 45 feet long, and had a battery of teeth each 6 inches long in its enormous jaws. Like Allosaurus, it walked on its hind legs, and the sharp claws on its front feet could grip like a vise. It could run at great speed and few creatures were safe from it. It spent its time killing, eating and sleeping. There is a skeleton of Tyrannosaurus Rex in the American Museum of Natural History in New York City.

One of the victims of the King of the Tyrants was Trachodon. This was a very large plant-eating dinosaur with a broad ducklike bill. It looked something like an outsize kangaroo and

32

had long hind legs and a thick wide tail which it used as a paddle when it was swimming. The fingers of its small hands were webbed like a duck's foot. Trachodon had no teeth in the front of its bill but it had 1,000 teeth on each side of its jaws; they were arranged in two rows of 500, so that altogether it had 2,000 teeth! It lived mainly in water but came onto dry land to lay its eggs, and then it had to keep a sharp lookout for Tyrannosaurus. The mummy of a trachodon was found in Montana in 1908, dried up and leathery but otherwise in perfect condition.

To protect themselves from the giant flesh-eaters, some of the vegetarian dinosaurs of the Jurassic Period developed a kind of armor. The best known of these is Stegosaurus. This reptile was up to 30 feet long and had a small head and four stout legs. Its armor consisted of two rows of bony plates set edgewise along its back, and long sharp spines on its tail. Stegosaurus had three "brains"! The one in its head was only as big as a billiard ball; another was placed in the spinal cord at the shoulder; and the third at the bottom of the hips. The two extra "brains" controlled the movement of the legs and tail. They did not, however, help Stegosaurus to last any longer than other type of dinosaur.

33

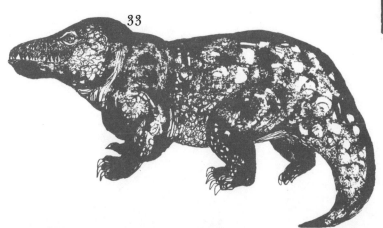

An armored dinosaur from the Cretaceous Period was Triceratops. It looked rather like a tank, with its thick body 25 feet long, its broad rounded feet, and the way it walked on all fours. There was a bony ruff protecting its neck, and three horns sticking out from its face, the horn on the nose being shorter than the other two. Each eye was guarded by an overhanging piece of bone. Triceratops was a fierce fighter in spite of being a vegetarian.

In 1822, the wife of an amateur paleontologist found some strange-looking teeth in Cretaceous rocks in Sussex, England. They turned out to belong to a kind of extinct reptile that had been unknown up to that time. As the teeth looked like those of a modern iguana lizard, this reptile was given the name Iguanodon. Several skeletons of the same creature were later found in a coal mine in Belgium. Iguanodon stood upright, with its head about 15 feet from the ground, and looked rather like a massive lizard. It was a harmless vegetarian. Near where the skeletons were found was an imprint of a tail where one of them had sat down to rest.

In the Mesozoic Era dinosaurs were the lords of the land but the air was ruled by flying reptiles. One of these creatures was

34

Pterodactyl, which means Wing Finger. Its wings were similar to those of a bat; it had a membrane stretching between the front and back limbs, supported by the bones of the front limb and an enormously long outer finger. Some members of the family had long bony jaws like beaks and were provided with teeth. Pterodactyls were agile in the air but much less so on the ground. They had owl-like eyes, so they probably flew at night. The smaller pterodactyls lived on insects, and the larger ones caught fish in their long beaks.

One of the largest creatures ever to fly in the Cretaceous Period was Pteranodon. It had a birdlike beak with no teeth, and a bony crest stuck out from the back of its head. As it had no tail, it probably steered with this crest and its legs. Its wing spread was 25 feet, and it must have looked like a witch as it flew and glided through the air. Remains of pteranodon have been found in western Kansas. It is important to remember that these flying reptiles were not birds — for one thing, they had no feathers — and they did not develop into birds. They died out just as the dinosaurs did.

Before describing the sea reptiles, we must meet one of the detectives whose clues have helped us to know so much about

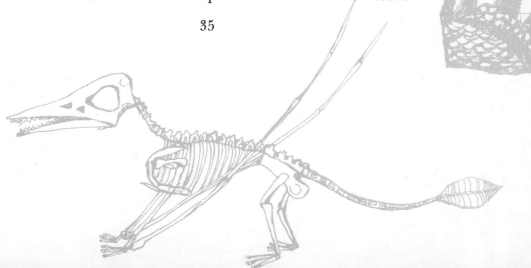

these creatures. In the British Museum of Natural History at South Kensington, there is a portrait of a jolly looking lady dressed in the clothes of the early nineteenth century. She is holding a hammer in one hand, and a basket of specimens hangs over her arm. On the ground beside her is her dog. Her name is Mary Anning and she was born in 1799.

Mary Anning was not an expert in paleontology. Her father was a carpenter at Lyme Regis in Dorset, England, and his hobby was collecting fossils from the seacoast, where ammonites and belemnites were common. (These are two extinct kinds of cephalopods: the former built their shells in a series of chambers, some straight or gently curved, others elaborately spiraled; the latter were dart-shaped.)

Mary used to help her father and grew quite skilled at finding fossils and prying them from the rocks in order to sell them as curios. When her father died in 1810, Mary continued her fossil-hunting so as to make a little extra money for her mother.

One day when she was twelve years old, she made the first of the many discoveries which were to make her famous. She was working with her hammer on some rocks near Lyme

38

Church when she unearthed some bones which she thought were those of a crocodile. What they turned out to be were the bones of Ichthyosaurus, one of the best known fish reptiles of the Mesozoic Era. Mary Anning was the first person ever to find ichthyosaurus fossils, and this was such an important discovery that it alone would have made her famous. But she did not stop there. She seemed to have a genius for finding such things, and during her lifetime she discovered remains of plesiosaurs, pterodactyls and several more ichthyosaurs. Mary Anning died in 1847. Her name will always stand out in the story of paleontology.

What were these sea reptiles like? Plesiosaur was like a giant turtle, up to 50 feet long, with a long neck, a short tail and paddlelike legs. People who believe in the Loch Ness Monster think that it is probably a form of plesiosaur which by some strange chance did not become extinct.

Pliosaurus was a kind of plesiosaur with a thick body and a very long neck, and it propelled itself along the surface of the sea with its four paddle-shaped limbs. Its head was from 4 to 6 feet long, and it had very sharp teeth. Another species, Kronosaurus, developed a skull nearly 10 feet long.

39

Mosasaurus was a fierce sea dragon. It grew to a length of 25 feet and had a head like a lizard's. The king of the turtles was Archelon, which weighed nearly 3 tons. It had a huge beak like a parrot's and it lived on shellfish which it caught in shallow waters.

Ichthyosaurus, Mary Anning's first great find, was a reptile that looked more like a fish than any of the others. It resembled a modern shark but was much longer than any variety we know. Ichthyosaurus had a long snout, huge eyes and a slender jaw well supplied with teeth. Instead of laying its eggs on land, the female kept them inside her body, and when they were hatched the young ones appeared alive. Skeletons of ichthyosaurs were found near Stuttgart in Germany, perfectly preserved in a slab of slate, and there were the skeletons of several young ones inside their bodies.

Although we have said that flying reptiles were not the ancestors of birds, there were some flying creatures of the Mesozoic Era that were distantly related to birds. One of these was Archaeopteryx, which means Ancient Wing. The first skeleton

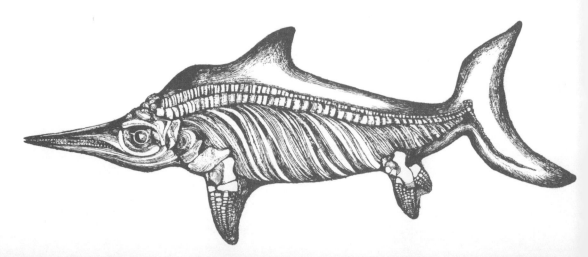

of archaeopteryx was found in 1861 in Jurassic rocks in Germany. The slab which contains the skeleton was bought by the British Museum. There is another specimen in the Berlin Natural History Museum. These "birds" had sharp teeth instead of bills, and sharp claws on their wings. They had tails like lizards but with feathers on them. The first birds were about the size of crows and probably could not fly very well. They spent most of their time climbing and scrambling up and down the trunks of trees.

Now we come to the Time of the Great Dying at the end of the Mesozoic Era when many of these creatures became extinct. All that were left were those which later developed into lizards, and crocodiles, turtles, birds and mammals. Life on earth began to find its balance again when, at the end of the Age of Reptiles, mammals became prominent and reached a far higher level of development than any other creature that so far had lived. (A mammal is a vertebrate with warm blood and soft fur or hair. The mother, instead of laying and hatching eggs, brings forth her babies alive and feeds them with milk from her own body.)

41

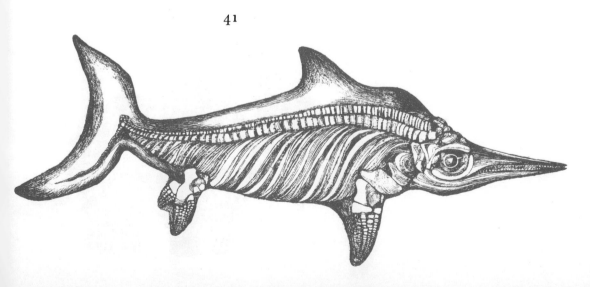

Chapter Four

THE AGE OF MAMMALS

THE MESOZOIC ERA was followed by the Cenozoic Era, which is also called the Age of Mammals. It began about 70 million years ago and lasted until one million years ago. During this time mammals grew common and developed into most of the groups that exist today, but also into others which have become extinct. Lands and seas became much as we know them and great mountain ranges appeared.

Cenozoic, you will remember, means Recent Life. The divisions into which this era is split are different from the others. Part of the time is covered by one period called the Tertiary (or Third). The Tertiary Period is divided into five Epochs, the names of which are all based on the Greek word *kainos* or *ceno*, meaning recent.

The earliest epoch is the Paleocene, or Ancient Dawn of the Recent. Next, the Eocene Epoch, the Dawn of the Recent.

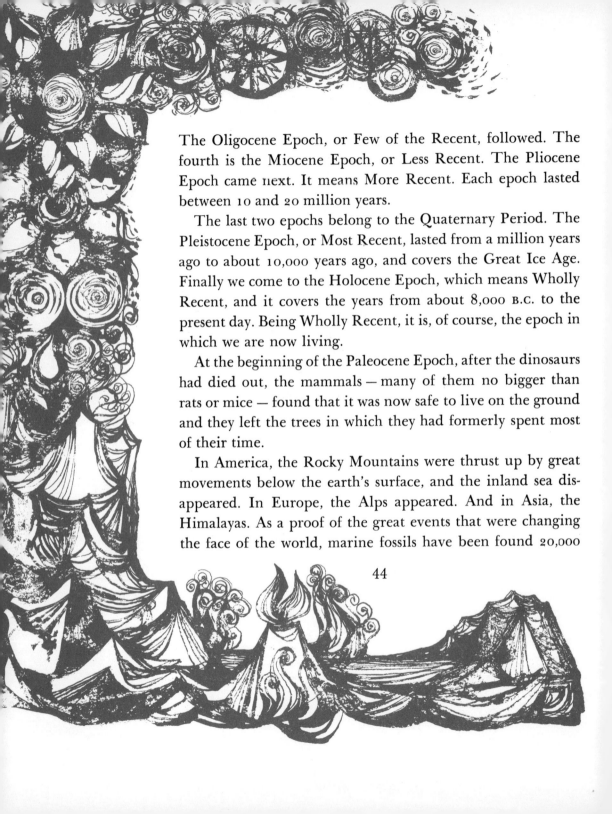

The Oligocene Epoch, or Few of the Recent, followed. The fourth is the Miocene Epoch, or Less Recent. The Pliocene Epoch came next. It means More Recent. Each epoch lasted between 10 and 20 million years.

The last two epochs belong to the Quaternary Period. The Pleistocene Epoch, or Most Recent, lasted from a million years ago to about 10,000 years ago, and covers the Great Ice Age. Finally we come to the Holocene Epoch, which means Wholly Recent, and it covers the years from about 8,000 B.C. to the present day. Being Wholly Recent, it is, of course, the epoch in which we are now living.

At the beginning of the Paleocene Epoch, after the dinosaurs had died out, the mammals — many of them no bigger than rats or mice — found that it was now safe to live on the ground and they left the trees in which they had formerly spent most of their time.

In America, the Rocky Mountains were thrust up by great movements below the earth's surface, and the inland sea disappeared. In Europe, the Alps appeared. And in Asia, the Himalayas. As a proof of the great events that were changing the face of the world, marine fossils have been found 20,000

44

feet high in the Himalayan rocks. There were also violent out-
bursts from volcanoes. Although the climate varied from epoch
to epoch, it was generally much warmer than it is today. Later
in the era, cold winds began to blow from the polar regions
and the heat grew less.

Plants and trees that we should recognize today appeared.
Hills were covered with grass, there were rolling plains and
forests of oak and maple trees, and the earth teemed with life
of all kinds.

The early mammals began to change, too. Some animals that
had lived on plants and insects took up hunting and ate what
they killed. Some of them began to look like the animals of
today. Baluchitherium, from the Oligocene Epoch, was an
ancient ancestor of the rhinoceros. Its remains have been found
in Baluchistan, in Asia. It was the largest land mammal that
ever lived, 18 feet high and 27 feet long. If you can imagine a
double-decker bus turned into a rhinoceros, you will get some
idea of its size!

During the Eocene Epoch the earliest ancestor of the horse
lived in Europe and North America. It is called Eohippus, or
Dawn Horse, though its correct name is Hyracotherium. It was

45

about as big as a fox terrier and lived in swampy forests. Its teeth were only fit for pulling at leaves. Eohippus was different from the modern horse, not only in size but also because it had toes — 3 on the hind feet and 4 on the front.

By the Oligocene Epoch, the horse had grown larger — about as big as a Saint Bernard dog. It had 3 toes on each foot. It is called Mesohippus, or Middle Horse.

In the Miocene Epoch, Merychippus had 3 toes on each foot but used only the middle one for running. And in the Pliocene Epoch, Pliohippus had only one toe visible, the outer pair being covered with skin.

In the Pleistocene Epoch, further changes brought a horse looking much like those of today. It was called Equus. The central toe had hardened into a tough hoof; the others had shrunk to splint bones.

Elephants have an interesting history, too. Although they are now among the biggest mammals, their first ancestor was a little creature from the Eocene Epoch called Moeritherium. It was less than 3 feet high and had neither tusks nor trunk, but it was able to grasp things with its upper lip. In the Oligocene Epoch, these animals became larger and two of their teeth

grew into large tusks. But small as they were, they had no trunks. It was only when their heads were too far from the ground and their tusks too long for them to reach their food that their trunk began to develop from their upper lips. Then they could reach with their trunk beyond the point of the tusks in order to get food and suck up water.

Among the late Cenozoic animals were a camel with a neck as long as a giraffe's, and a giant "pig" over 10 feet long and higher than a man. Dinotherium, a relative of the elephant, had tusks that curved backward like the claws of a cat. In South America there were huge ground sloths and armadillos. Diprotodon, in Australia, was a kind of wombat as big as a rhinoceros.

All the animals so far described were herbivores and ate only plants. And they were the prey of the carnivores, the flesh-eaters. The best known carnivores of the late Cenozoic Era were the great cats usually called sabre-toothed tigers because of their long upper canine teeth. Smilodon, an American great cat, must have been magnificent to look at, but its huge, stabbing fangs were deadly dangerous.

Diatryma was a carnivorous bird which was unable to fly.

47

It was taller than a man, had stout legs, and a large head with a beak that ended in a sharp hook — very useful for tearing its victims to pieces!

But these animals, in spite of their size and ferocity, were not the most important creatures living on the earth. There was a group of small animals living in trees and feeding on insects, the ancestors of lemurs, tarsiers and monkeys. One of these, the Tarsioid, has a present-day relative called the Spectral Tarsier which lives in the East Indies. One very important thing about it was that its eyes were not set one on either side of its head — as a cat's or a dog's are — but both were in the front of the head, like a man's. They could be brought to focus on a single point, giving a deep and solid picture. None of the larger mammals had eyes which they could use in this way. The tarsioid used its front feet as hands, and its fingers had nails rather than claws. But — and this is the most important thing of all — the tarsioid could use its hands, eyes and brain together, all acting in partnership. Although the tarsioid was nothing like anything that we could call man, it was probably the earliest sign that something was going to happen — a sign that just being big and fierce and acting without being able to think was not enough. In time there developed a higher order of mammals which included lemurs, tarsiers and monkeys and is called Primate. Man is a primate.

But before we follow the development of the mammals from the first primates to the first men, we must look at the strange things that were happening to the world during the Cenozoic Era.

Chapter Five

THE GREAT ICE AGE

THE PLEISTOCENE EPOCH, which began about a million years ago, saw great changes come to the world: winds grew sharp and cold, grasses were shorter, forests shrank, and evergreen trees were more common.

Then came the ice. Vast white sheets of it slowly spread from the polar regions until they completely covered Greenland, Siberia, northern Europe and much of both North America and South America. Snow fell and moisture was trapped in the ice so that the level of the seas fell. And land which had been under water for millions of years reappeared.

There was a land bridge from Alaska to Siberia, and another between North and South America. Animals traveled from continent to continent, seeking to escape the cold. Some of the less hardy species died out altogether.

In the first 100,000 years of the Pleistocene Epoch, ice sheets covered a third of the earth's surface, and places which had previously had warm and gentle climates suffered harsh and almost endless winter.

Then the glaciers retreated and the warmth returned. But the cold came again, and this pattern was repeated four times. Each one of these invasions of great glaciers is called a Glacial Period, and together they form the Great Ice Age. It was during this time that the land part of the earth's surface became the shape it is today. The warm times in between were much longer than the ice invasions themselves.

The latest retreat of ice began about 20,000 years ago and is still going on. But the Great Ice Age may not be completely over, and it is possible, though not in our lifetime, that either the ice at present covering the Poles may disappear altogether, or it may once again creep downward and plunge the world of the future into a fifth Glacial Period.

Although nobody knows the reason for these tremendous changes in climate, we do know the difference they made to the living things that inhabited the world. There are many fossil remains from the Pleistocene Epoch, and whole animals have been found, frozen and preserved, in the Arctic snow and ice. A huge, hairy elephant called a Mammoth was revealed by a fall in the bank of a river on Wrangel Island in the Arctic Circle. It has been in its "deep freeze" for perhaps 20,000 years, but its flesh was so fresh that it was eaten by dogs.

52

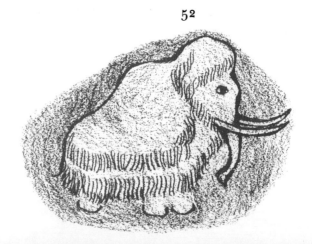

During the Fourth Glacial advance, England was cold and bare. Herds of woolly mammoths roamed along the valley of the Thames. Their bones have been found in Kent's Cavern, near Torquay in southwest England — the largest prehistoric cave in that country. Kent's Cavern was first excavated in 1825 by a priest named Father MacEnery. In addition to mammoth bones, he found — at different levels — remains of the saber-toothed tiger, the Great Irish Elk, cave hyena, woolly rhinoceros and cave bear, the latter a great ferocious beast that also lived in caves and rock shelters in France, Germany, Switzerland and Spain.

During the long warm times between the Glacial stages, new kinds of animals moved into Europe from the tropical lands of the south. Herds of game from Africa crossed the land bridge which is now the Strait of Gibraltar. They also came from Tunis to Sicily and Italy, all joined together at that time. There were hippopotamuses wallowing in the rivers and lions and hyenas hunting in the forests of northwest Europe.

In North America, the new mammals lived on the prairies; camels and wild horses, bison with horns 6 feet long, stabbing cats and wolves, and smaller creatures such as the weasel, otter and badger.

53

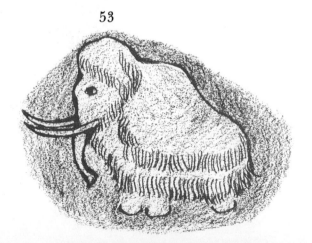

One of the birds of the Pleistocene Epoch was Diornis. It was like a giant moa, more than 10 feet tall, and lived in New Zealand. Aepyornis was smaller than Diornis but it laid the biggest eggs ever known. Fossil eggshells, bigger than footballs and capable of holding two gallons of liquid, have been found in Madagascar.

As these shaggy animals and giant birds gradually became extinct in the final years of the Pleistocene Epoch, great num-

54

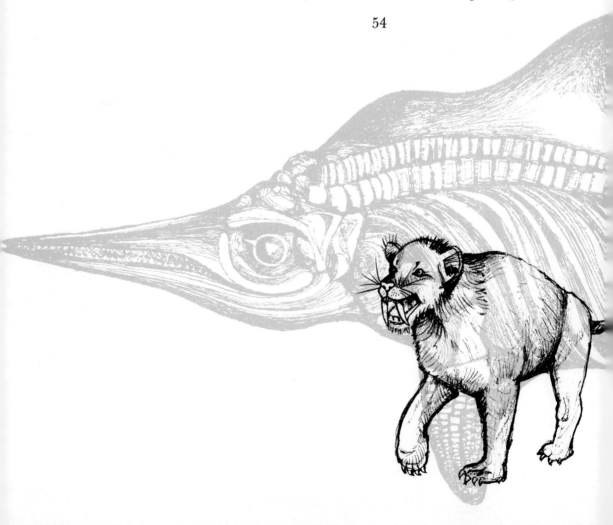

bers of animals of a more modern type took possession of the earth. They were much the same in form as those we know today, and during the last 20,000 years there has been little change in the shapes, habits and varieties of such animals as the lion, tiger, elephant and bison.

The stage is almost set for the appearance of man on the scene, but before we raise the curtain on that we must hear something about Evolution.

55

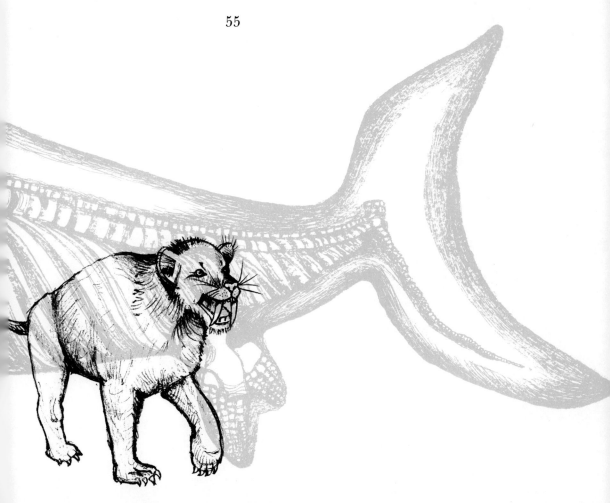

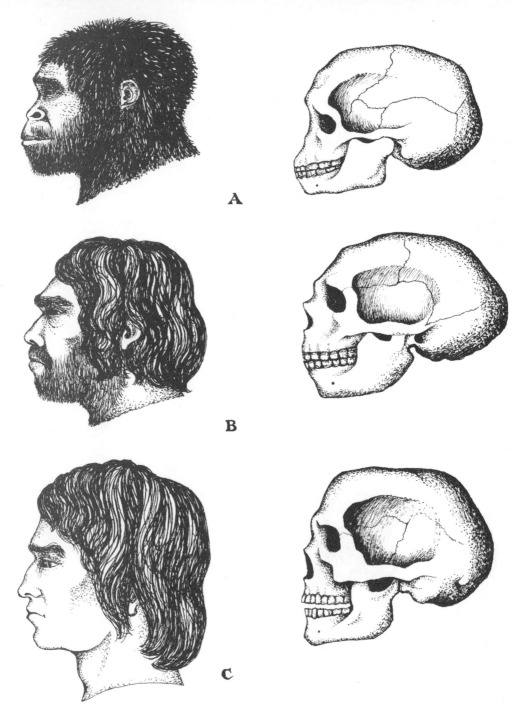

Fossil Man. A Group of Skulls, oldest at the top, showing changes in skull of fossil man

A. Australopithecus   B. Neanderthal man   C. Cro-magnon man

Chapter Six

APES AND NEAR MEN

DURING THE MILLIONS of years of the earth's history, we have seen that plants and animals have changed a great deal. Many have died out altogether, but others have developed in various ways in order to fit themselves to changes in their living conditions. These changes were very gradual and the process which makes them happen is called Evolution.

No two plants or animals are exactly alike, and there are always some with certain characteristics that make them able to survive better than others.

There has been a gradual succession of changes in the various forms of living creatures from the earliest living matter to the animals of the present day, and of the many types that these changes produced, those which had the best chance of survival lasted, while others died out. These ideas were introduced by Charles Darwin in his book, *On the Origin of Species by Means of Natural Selection*, in 1859.

Charles Darwin was born in England in 1809. When he was a boy, his family thought him rather stupid, for it seemed to them that Charles spent too much of his time observing the habits of worms and beetles and the formation of rocks. When he was twenty-two, he went on a voyage around the world in H.M.S. *Beagle*, which lasted for five years. During that time he was able to study the plants, animals and rocks in such places as the Galapagos Islands, Australia, Tasmania and New Zealand. In 1840, he wrote a book about the trip. It was called *Zoology of the Voyage of the Beagle*.

His next book was *The Descent of Man*, published in 1871. Many people thought that Darwin was saying that men were descended from monkeys, and they did not like that idea at all. Actually he did not say anything of the kind. Darwin's belief was that both monkeys and men had a common ancestor. Nowadays most people agree that he was right, and his ideas of evolution are accepted. Darwin died in 1882, having spent most of his life studying and writing about his theories.

We have already met some of man's early ancestors among the primates, the group of animals to which man belongs. In the modern world our closest relatives are the gorillas, chimpanzees, orangutans and gibbons. The next nearest are the monkeys, and behind them the tarsiers with their wistful faces and huge, staring eyes. Finally, at the bottom of the list, come the lemurs, now found only on the island of Madagascar, with their foxlike snouts and eyes spaced widely apart.

There are not nearly as many fossils of primates as there are of other animals, but the remains of early apes of the Miocene and Pliocene epochs have been found, and also of the first human beings, men who could make and use tools, who had lived in the Pleistocene Epoch.

But that is getting on with the story too quickly. We must first go back to the Oligocene Epoch in Egypt. There, in a dried-up lake, were found a jawbone and some teeth belonging to quite a small animal which was almost, but not quite, an ape. It is called Parapithecus, or Near Ape.

Another jawbone found in Egypt came from a slightly larger monkeylike creature in a more advanced stage of evolution. Somewhere about this time — about 45 million years ago — these animals developed in two different ways: one group into monkeys, and the other group into apes. No one can be quite sure when and how this branching off took place, but we do know that in the Miocene Epoch there were apes living in Africa that were quite different from monkeys and that were the ancestors of the modern ape families.

In Kenya, near Lake Victoria, jawbones and pieces of a skull were discovered which belonged to an animal smaller than, but similar to, a chimpanzee. It is called Proconsul. Another kind

59

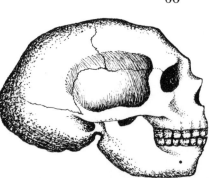

of tree ape called Dryopithecus lived in Europe and Asia. Some scientists believe that this chimpanzeelike animal was a common ancestor of both apes and men, but others think that men's ancestors had appeared before Dryopithecus. Not enough teeth and bones have yet been discovered to prove who is right, so the question is still unsettled.

Although the next creature to be described cannot be called a true man, he was very near one. During recent years many important fossil remains have been discovered. The main areas where these menlike apes saw the light of day are Africa and Asia, but there is evidence that they later migrated to Europe. No fossil remains of these early men have been found in either America or Australia. The early Pleistocene man-ape is called Australopithecus. This name has nothing to do with Australia. Austral is a Latin word which means southern, so Australopithecus means Southern Ape.

What we know of Australopithecus has been put together from the evidence of a skull found in a limestone cave in Bechuanaland in 1925. The skull had the facial outline of a chimpanzee but the brain and teeth were almost those of a man. Professor Raymond Dart, of Johannesburg, thought that it was nearer to man than any other fossil discovered up to that time. There was a lot of argument about this theory, and then

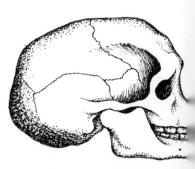

more finds were made in South Africa in 1936 and 1938. One of them was by a schoolboy who saw a skull sticking out from a rock as he was climbing over the top of a hill. He pried it loose and took it away with him. Dr. Robert Broom of the Transvaal Museum in Pretoria, who had himself found a similar skull, heard of the boy's find and was eager to examine it. He hurried off to the boy's school, wondering if there would be anything left for him to examine! After all, it was unlikely that the boy would realize the scientific value of his find, and he might have thrown it away or used it as a football. To Dr. Broom's great relief, however, the boy took out of his pocket four of the most important teeth ever seen in the world's history. . . .

When all the new finds had been fully examined, it became clear that Australopithecus had stood and walked upright, not with the crouched-up shuffle of apes. He and his companions had probably lived in caves, hunted and gathered food such as small animals, and nuts and berries. So he was no longer completely apelike, though not completely human. It is not yet clear whether or not he was human enough to use some kind of tool.

In 1959, a skull was found in the Olduvai Gorge, Tanganyika, by the wife of Professor L. S. B. Leakey, together with a

61

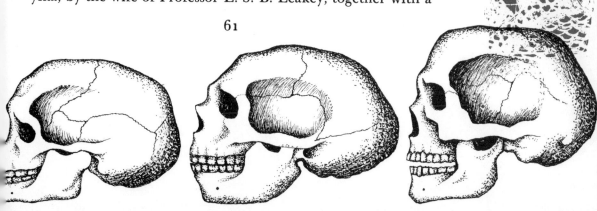

number of pebble tools. The great size of the teeth has led to Zinjanthropus, its scientific name, being given the nickname of Nutcracker Man. It is thought that he lived roughly at the same time as Australopithecus, in the Lower Pleistocenc Epoch, and that he was the first creature to supplement his diet of wild vegetables with meat — shown by the discovery of the bones of small animals, broken open so that the marrow could be extracted.

In 1961, two more fossil finds were made in the same lakeside hunting ground of early man, and these may be even more important than Zinjanthropus. One is the bones, jawbone and teeth of a child who lived even earlier, perhaps, than Australopithecus; the second is the cap of the skull of a creature who lived at the same time as the Java Man, who comes next in the story. The site of these new finds contained many stone tools and the remains of tortoises and catfish.

These new discoveries make the Olduvai Gorge one of the most important archaeological sites in Africa, and further discoveries are expected to help build an almost complete picture of the way these humanlike people used to live. They will also add weight to the belief that true man first saw the light of day in Africa.

Until Professor Leakey's discoveries we have had to go to the Far East for the first known ancestor of real man.

The remains of this creature were discovered between 1890 and 1891 in a village in Java in the East Indies by a Dutchman named Eugène Dubois. Java Man, as he is called, though his scientific name is Pithecanthropus erectus, or Erect Ape Man, lived in the Pleistocene Epoch. He, too, walked upright, his forehead sloped back, and his brain, though larger than an ape's, was smaller than a man's. There was a great deal of argument at the time of this discovery about whether Dubois' find was really a man or a kind of ape, but since 1936 more discoveries have been made in Java, and Java Man's place in the story of man has been established.

Another "dawn man" is known to have lived in the Far East. Just one tooth was found by a Canadian scientist in a Chinese village west of Pekin. This first clue came to light in 1927, and during the next ten years further searches brought the remains of 45 similar men, together with the bones of animals and primitive stone tools. The bones of Pekin Man, or Pithecanthropus pekinensis, were like those of Java Man. He lived between a quarter and half a million years ago. He was perhaps the first toolmaker and he also knew how to use fire. The re-

63

mains of hearths were discovered with burned charcoal and nearby the charred bones of animals, which showed that he knew how to cook his food. Rather more gruesome were the broken fossil skulls of humans that were lying near the hearths. It is thought that Pekin Man was a cannibal and had cracked open the skulls so that the brains could be taken out and cooked.

Now our search for the earliest men brings us back to Europe. We really know very little about them because all that has been found is a jawbone and some teeth. These were discovered in a sandpit near Heidelberg, Germany, in 1907. Heidelberg Man dates from about the middle of the Pleistocene Epoch, and he is known as the First European.

From 1908 until 1953, there was another candidate for the position of the First European. The story of Piltdown Man is rather like a detective story on its own. It is also the story of a hoax that took in, not only most ordinary people, but also some of the greatest scientists. It all began when a lawyer named Charles Dawson, who was very interested in archaeology, claimed to have discovered pieces of a skull and some teeth in a gravel pit near Piltdown in Sussex, England. Later, in another part of the same district, more pieces of skull and half a lower

64

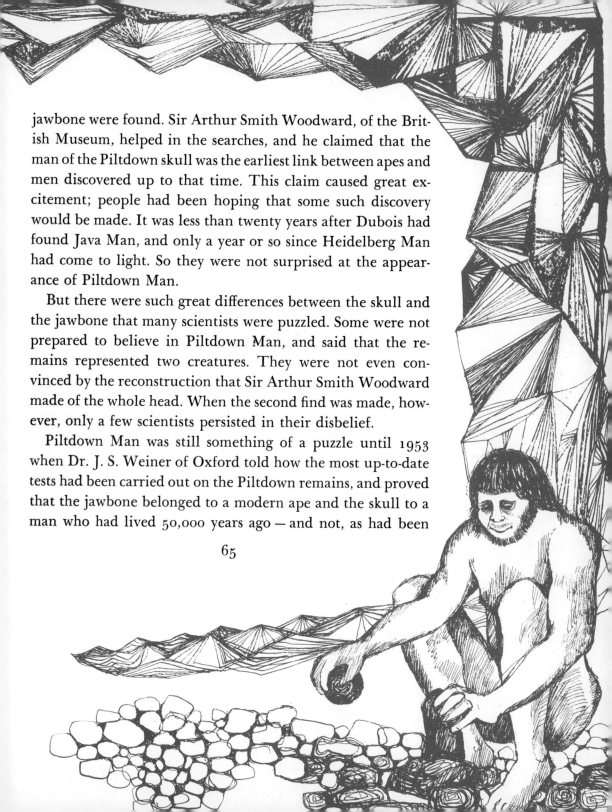

jawbone were found. Sir Arthur Smith Woodward, of the British Museum, helped in the searches, and he claimed that the man of the Piltdown skull was the earliest link between apes and men discovered up to that time. This claim caused great excitement; people had been hoping that some such discovery would be made. It was less than twenty years after Dubois had found Java Man, and only a year or so since Heidelberg Man had come to light. So they were not surprised at the appearance of Piltdown Man.

But there were such great differences between the skull and the jawbone that many scientists were puzzled. Some were not prepared to believe in Piltdown Man, and said that the remains represented two creatures. They were not even convinced by the reconstruction that Sir Arthur Smith Woodward made of the whole head. When the second find was made, however, only a few scientists persisted in their disbelief.

Piltdown Man was still something of a puzzle until 1953 when Dr. J. S. Weiner of Oxford told how the most up-to-date tests had been carried out on the Piltdown remains, and proved that the jawbone belonged to a modern ape and the skull to a man who had lived 50,000 years ago — and not, as had been

65

claimed by the finders 500,000 years ago. The ape's jawbone had been artificially colored to look like the skull, and the teeth had been filed so that they would appear to have worn down in the same way that a man's teeth would have.

Whoever thought up this practical joke and carried it out by planting the fake clues certainly fooled a lot of people and for a long time. It is not known who was responsible for it, though books have been written blaming one or another of the suspects. Piltdown Man can still be seen in the British Museum of Natural History, but in a case of his own, away from the true ancestors of mankind.

Heidelberg Man, you will remember, is called the First European. The First Englishman is Swanscombe Man. Part of a human skull was unearthed near Swanscombe in Kent, England, in 1935, together with some fine battle-axes. Other pieces came to light in 1955, but unfortunately none of the finds included a forehead, so we cannot be sure whether Swanscombe Man had a smooth brow like our own, or a low and prominent one like Neanderthal Man. This hunter of the Thames Valley lived in the early Pleistocene Epoch. There is some doubt, too,

66

as to whether his nickname is correct — according to some scientists it ought to be the First Englishwoman!

Neanderthal Man comes next in the story of man, though he seems to represent a separate line of development which became extinct at the end of the Middle Paleolithic Period. He was one of the inhabitants of Europe more than 130,000 years ago. His skull was first found in the Neander Valley in Germany in 1856, and he was perhaps a descendant of creatures like the ape men of Java and Pekin. Other skeletons have since been found in France, Belgium, Italy, the Channel Islands, Palestine, southern Russia, Siberia and North Africa. He was short and stocky, with a large and thick-boned skull, a receding forehead and no chin. He generally lived in caves and made excellent tools of flint. Neanderthal Man died out at the beginning of the Fourth Glacial Period.

We must interrupt the story of man at this point to examine more closely the things he used to help him to hunt and kill, dig and scrape.

You will have noticed that, with the remains of the men found since Pekin Man, there have also been tools nearby. Primitive tools and weapons have, in fact, been found in much

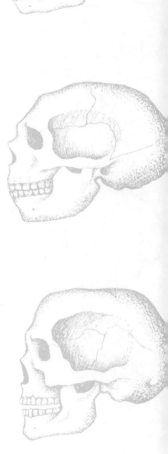

greater quantities than the bones of the men who made them. Archaeologists consider them of great importance. They have been made of different materials, in different sizes and shapes, and they give us a good deal of information about man's progress, the way he lived and died, his customs and habits.

Let us refer again to the calendar of earth history. We have now reached the Pleistocene Epoch, which began about a million years ago and lasted until 10,000 years ago. This period of time is also called the Paleolithic Age, or Old Stone Age. The earliest part of it, the Lower Paleolithic Age, lasted until about 220,000 years ago, until the Third Glacial Period. This was the age of Java Man and Pekin Man. Pekin Man's tools were large and rough, and it is possible that his method of stoneworking spread from the Far East to Europe and Africa.

The second part of this period is the Middle Paleolithic Age, and covered the time between the Third and Fourth Glacial Periods. Neanderthal Man lived at this time, and his flintworking was a great improvement on that of earlier man. He also used skins for clothing.

The third and last division of the Paleolithic Age is the

68

Upper Paleolithic Age, or Late Old Stone Age. It lasted from about 60,000 years ago until roughly 10,000 years ago, the end of the Pleistocene Epoch. By then, Old Stone Age men were making fine stone tools and weapons and small and delicate things such as bone needles, harpoons and arrowheads. Their artists engraved on bone tools and painted on cave walls.

What are perhaps the earliest tools of the Pleistocene Epoch are called Eoliths, or Dawn Stones. They are stones which appear to have been used by men as tools although not specially made for the purpose. Benjamin Harrison — who had the same name as the twenty-third President of the United States — was the first man to discover eoliths and to suggest what they were used for. He was a village shopkeeper who lived at Ightham, near Maidstone in Kent, England. He was born in 1837, the year in which Queen Victoria came to the throne. Benjamin Harrison's hobby was collecting relics of the ancient men of Kent, and he used to explore the fields and gravel pits near his home. He discovered eoliths in some gravel on a farm in 1865, and one of the first he found is now set in a memorial tablet in Ightham Church.

There is still some doubt about whether or not eoliths really were the first made tools. Some of these chipped flints certainly were not, but others may have been. Eoliths will always remain something of a puzzle.

When Stone Age men began to make their stone implements, they chipped the pieces of stone to the shape they wanted. Flints, found in chalk, were best for their purpose, and "factories" have been found where the making was carried out. One of the best known of the mines from which flint was excavated (much later in the Stone Age) is on a heath near Brandon in Norfolk, England, and is called Grime's Graves. Here there are circular pits or shallow mines from which the flints were taken. To judge from the objects found there — anvil stones, heaps of chips, animal and human bones — it must have been a busy and important place. You can descend into one of the pits and see the galleries hollowed out by the workmen. The picks they used were the antlers of deer, and one of them still shows the fingerprints of the miner who handled it.

There were two ways of making flint tools. One was by chipping long flakes from a lump of flint and using the core

70

that was left as a scraper or battle ax. These are known as core tools. Flake tools were also made. The flakes were chipped off a large piece of flint, and the flakes themselves used as spear-heads and knives; the unwanted core was then thrown away. The edges of all the tools were chipped all around, in order to make them sharp. It is this chipping that enables us to recognize Paleolithic tools. They are often found in gravel pits or turned up by the plow in fields with a chalky subsoil. A search in such places might well bring to light a battle ax that had last been touched by a man living more than 50,000 years ago.

The name of Jacques Boucher de Perthes will always be remembered in connection with the flint tools of the Old Stone Age. He was a French Customs Officer who became interested in the old tools and bones thrown up when the Somme Canal was being dredged. In 1837, he turned his attention to the gravel pits near where he lived and found hundreds of flaked flint axes and bones of reindeer, bears and mammoths. He believed that the tools were the same age as the bones and that his collection showed how man had advanced from his first rough strokes on flint to making the smooth and polished tools

71

of later times. But, as so often happens when new ideas are put forward, nobody believed him. He was thought to be a ridiculous crank.

Boucher de Perthes was undismayed, and in 1847 a book about his finds and his museum was published. This did not help either. Scientists said that he was a dreamer or a fraud. They argued that since there were no fossil men, how could the tools belong to the time of fossil mammals?

It was not until 1859 that de Perthes's ideas were taken seriously, first by two English scientists who visited his museum and examined his collection carefully. Afterward they declared that they believed he was right. His discoveries proved that there were men living in the times when the mammoth, woolly rhinoceros and cave bear roamed the countrysides of Europe.

Boucher de Perthes lived in Abbeville, France, and the kind of tools he found belong to the Abbeville Culture of the Lower Paleolithic Age, though no remains of the men who made them have been found so far.

Between the Third and Fourth Glacial Periods, when the earth was warm, Neanderthal men wandered over Europe in families and hunted small game. Occasionally they would capture a hippopotamus or an elephant, and think themselves lucky to have food that would last for quite a long time. If they stayed in one place for any length of time, they would choose a site by a stream. They would protect themselves from the weather by building a screen of bushes or by fastening animal skins between two trees.

But at the beginning of the Fourth Glacial Period the bitter winds and icy weather made life very hard for the Neanderthal people. The mammoth and the woolly rhinoceros took the place of the animals they knew, and life was more dangerous, as well as more uncomfortable. It is also possible that they were attacked by a more advanced type of man. They sheltered in caves and holes, huddled around their fires and pulled their skins around them to keep warm. The floors of these caves are often littered with the burned and broken bones of animals

and with the tools they left behind when they moved or were chased away by a cave lion.

An interesting fact about Neanderthal Man is that he buried his dead, and skeletons have been found with tools beside them in the grave. This indicates that Neanderthal Man believed that the dead went to another world where they still had need of their earthly tools and weapons.

There are some caves in a valley near Le Moustier in France, in which Neanderthal men lived. Tools found there include sharp-edged scrapers for dressing skins, battle axes and spears. These implements belong to the Mousterian Culture. There is now a statue of Mousterian Man standing on a cliff top overlooking the valley, a permanent reminder of our ugly, shambling forerunners.

As Neanderthal Man was dying out in the Fourth Glacial Period another race of men came from Africa or Asia and settled in Europe. They were taller, stronger and more advanced than the Neanderthalers. They turned them out of their caves and forced them to retreat to regions where they

had no protection from the cold. So, after lasting for 100,000 years, Neanderthal Man gave way to, or was absorbed by, these new men from the east who were our first true ancestors.

We call them Homo sapiens, or Wise Men. Men of our own kind are different from all the other kinds of primates because they have a skeleton which is completely erect, lighter bones, brains which have developed in different areas, and improved powers of reasoning.

The entry of Homo sapiens was a very important change in the evolution of human beings.

75

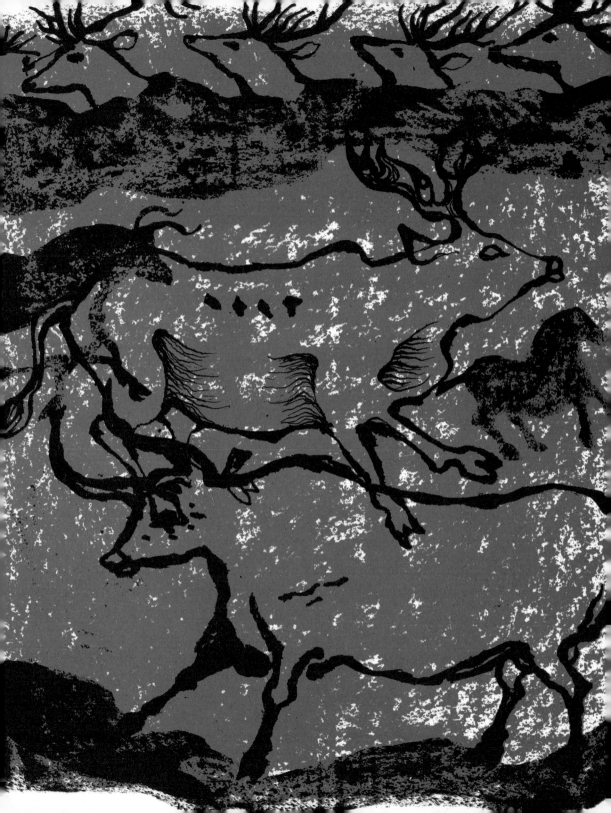

Chapter Seven

MEN OF THE OLD STONE AGE

IN 1868, WHEN some workmen were building a railway through the Vézère Valley in France, they found, at the bottom of a cliff, some chipped flints and animal bones. When an archaeologist named Edouard Lartet heard of these finds, he went to the valley and excavated in the rock shelter there.

He found five skeletons which had been buried at the back of the shelter, which was called Cro-Magnon. The skeletons were those of an old man, two young men, a woman and a child, and the bodies had been decorated with necklaces and ornaments made from shells and animals' teeth. Perhaps they had all been murdered during some religious ceremony, but in any case the skeletons were very well preserved. Cro-Magnon Man, as this species was called, was tall and strong, with a broad, high forehead, prominent cheekbones and a firm chin. He was not at all apelike in looks, and he was not a complete savage in his ways.

Four years before the Cro-Magnon skeletons were found, tools were discovered in another rock shelter called La Madeleine, a few miles away. One of these tools was a piece of mammoth bone with a drawing of a mammoth engraved on it. We call these tools Magdalenian, and the men who made them Magdalenian Men. Magdalenian Man used flints for scrapers and borers, and bone and ivory for his other implements. These people were widely scattered over Europe. They were great fishermen, as we know from their well-designed harpoons and fish-hooks, and they hunted the seal and the salmon.

In Great Britain, Magdalenian Man had what might be called a poor cousin whose tools have been found in the caves of Creswell Crags in Derbyshire, and other places.

There is a lot of argument about still another man who lived in Paleolithic times. Some skeletons found in a cave near the French–Italian border seemed to show that they had belonged to men whose features resembled those of Negroes rather than of Cro-Magnon Man. These first finds, made in 1874, were of two children with badly smashed skulls. In 1890, two more skeletons were found buried side by side, those of an old woman and a youth. These people belonged to Grimaldi Man, so called because Grimaldi is the family name of the Prince of

Monaco who was responsible for the later search. Some scientists think that Grimaldi Man made his way into Europe from Africa, while others say that such a thing is impossible because no similar remains have been found in North Africa. In any case, they argue, men enjoying a warm climate would not have been tempted to move northward into the frozen lands of Europe.

This argument, which has been going on for more than fifty years, will not be settled until more of Grimaldi Man's bones are found. What we can accept as fact is that there were a number of different races of men living in Europe over 30,000 years ago — some short, some tall, some with round heads, some with long ones, some with Negro-like features and some of a European type.

The Upper Paleolithic Age is divided according to the type of stone tools made by different tribes and races of men. Early man's way of making tools, weapons and ornaments — of building his homes and burying his dead — is called a Culture, which is named after the place where the relics have been found. We have already heard about the Magdalenian Culture. This was preceded by the Aurignacian Culture, named after a cave at Aurignac in France. The third great culture of

79

this time was the Solutrean, from the village of Solutré, also in France.

The main implement of the Solutrean Culture is a flint shaped rather like a laurel leaf, thin and flat and used for spears and arrowheads. The bones of 100,000 horses shot by men using bows and arrows were found at Solutré. There are models of clay bison, found in a cave in the Pyrénées, and wall paintings of horses, bison and ibex in another rock shelter, also possibly belonging to the same culture.

The most amazing discovery about the men who lived in Europe toward the end of the Great Ice Age was made in 1879 in a cave in northern Spain at a place called Altamira. Marcelino de Sautuola, a Spaniard, had taken his five-year-old daughter Maria with him on a fossil-hunting expedition in the cave. While her father was busy, little Maria decided to explore for herself in another part of the cave that was so low that no grown-up person had ever bothered to examine it. Suddenly her father heard her cry out that she could see bulls! He hurried over to her and found that she was looking at the roof of the cave. De Sautuola followed his daughter's gaze and there in the shadows he saw that a herd of bison had been painted on the roof in red and black. No one had set eyes on them for perhaps 30,000 years until Maria had taken her candle to the narrow opening of the 300-yard-long cave.

De Sautuola himself believed that the paintings had been done in the Old Stone Age, but once again the doubters would not agree with him. In time, however, other paintings were found in other places, and it was not possible that they could have been faked.

In 1895, some boys explored a narrow cave passage running into a hill at La Mouthe in the Vézère Valley, near the village of Les Eyzies, and found there drawings of horses, bison, reindeer, rhinoceroses and mammoths.

Children and dogs have been concerned with many of the findings which have been of such great help to archaeologists. The boy in South Africa who found the skull, Mary Anning and her many fossils of strange creatures, Maria de Sautuola and the cave paintings — and now we will hear of more.

Three brothers drifted up an underground river in 1912 and reached a cave with animal paintings on the walls. Leaving their boat, they continued on foot along a narrow tunnel which led them to another huge cave full of stalactites and stalagmites. From there the adventurous trio climbed through a hole in the roof into another small chamber, and there they found, behind a stalagmite, a tunnel so narrow that they could only wriggle along it with difficulty. It led to a series of passages and rooms, in one of which they discovered two statues of bison made of clay; and in the clay floor there were footprints made by Old

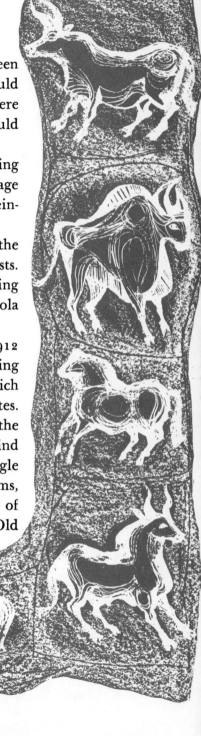

Stone Age men thousands of years before! Two years later the same boys found yet another cave in the hillside, again with prehistoric animals painted on the walls.

In 1922, an explorer named Norbert Casteret followed an underground river for nearly two miles under a hill in southern France and came to a cave in which there were clay statues of lions and a bear.

But the most wonderful cave of all was discovered in 1940, and again by boys! This one was in the Vézère Valley and is called Lascaux. A farmer had previously found a hole in the ground and had covered it with branches so that his cattle would not fall into it. Five schoolboys, climbing up the hill, suddenly found that Robot, their dog, was missing. He had disappeared down the hole, so the boys had to remove the farmer's covering and go down after their pet.

When they realized that they were in a cave passage, they decided to explore, but first they went home to get candles and ropes. The passage led to a large cavern with two other caves opening out from it. The walls were covered with paintings of enormous bulls, horses, deer, goats and bison. The paintings were well preserved and beautifully painted, probably by men

82

living between 15,000 and 20,000 years ago. Some of the animals were not painted but scratched on the walls, and all were full of life and movement — leaping, running, being hunted and killed.

The excited boys rushed away to get their schoolmaster to examine their find. He was so thrilled when he saw the marvellous sight that he immediately contacted a famous French archaeologist, a priest named Abbé Breuil, an expert in the art of the Old Stone Age, who died in 1961. A full exploration of the cave was made under the Abbé's supervision, and more wonderful paintings came to light.

The main chamber of the Lascaux Cave is oval, 100 feet long, 33 feet wide and 20 feet high. The largest of the bulls is 17 feet long. There is a frieze of little horses and a strange hunting scene containing a bird-faced man. The Abbé Breuil made copies of all the paintings and engravings, and their fame soon became worldwide. The cave was visited by thousands of people every year, and the guides included two of the boys who first discovered it, now grown men. In 1963, the cave was closed because a creeping fungus had attacked the pictures and they were losing their brilliance.

83

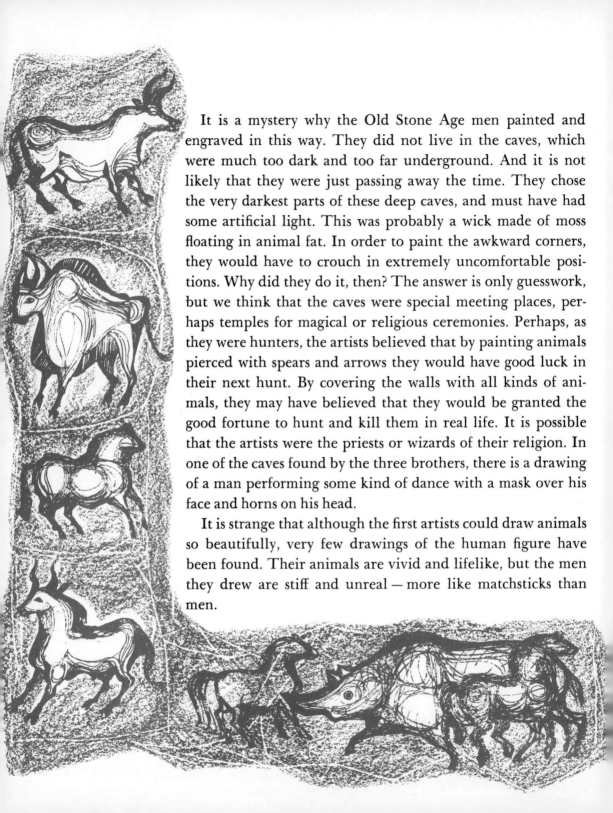

It is a mystery why the Old Stone Age men painted and engraved in this way. They did not live in the caves, which were much too dark and too far underground. And it is not likely that they were just passing away the time. They chose the very darkest parts of these deep caves, and must have had some artificial light. This was probably a wick made of moss floating in animal fat. In order to paint the awkward corners, they would have to crouch in extremely uncomfortable positions. Why did they do it, then? The answer is only guesswork, but we think that the caves were special meeting places, perhaps temples for magical or religious ceremonies. Perhaps, as they were hunters, the artists believed that by painting animals pierced with spears and arrows they would have good luck in their next hunt. By covering the walls with all kinds of animals, they may have believed that they would be granted the good fortune to hunt and kill them in real life. It is possible that the artists were the priests or wizards of their religion. In one of the caves found by the three brothers, there is a drawing of a man performing some kind of dance with a mask over his face and horns on his head.

It is strange that although the first artists could draw animals so beautifully, very few drawings of the human figure have been found. Their animals are vivid and lifelike, but the men they drew are stiff and unreal — more like matchsticks than men.

What happened to these Paleolithic artists? They seem to have disappeared completely from Europe at the end of the Fourth Glacial Period. We do not know whether they were conquered and killed off by a stronger race of people or made into slaves; whether they moved to another part of the world or whether they just died out. Whatever happened, the next men we are to hear about had no connection with Cro-Magnon Man of Aurignac, La Madeleine and Solutré. They had no interest in cave paintings and made no use of the caves.

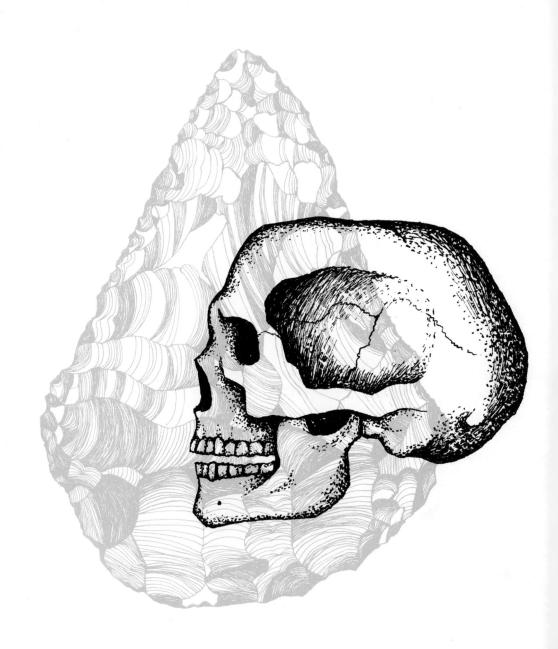

SKULL OF A CRO-MAGNON MALE: Flint of a Palaeolithic Age

Chapter Eight

MEN OF THE NEW STONE AGE

As THE LAST Glacial Period came to an end Europe slowly became warmer and plants and trees grew again on what had been bare or grassy land. Those animals that preferred a colder climate gradually moved northward, and as the warmth replaced the cold, the slow process of civilization was quickened. Old Stone Age painters were succeeded by new races of men who probably came from the south and the east.

In 1887, relics of these men were found in caves at Mas d'Azil near Toulouse in France. There were flat harpoons made from the horns of stags, the bones of the red deer and the wild boar, and pebbles painted with strange patterns in red ochre. Although no one knows for sure what they were used for, it is possible that they were the first coins or the first attempts at writing or perhaps they were connected with religious ceremonies and had magical qualities. These people belonged to the Azilian Culture, which was perhaps a development of the Magdalenian.

Relics of another race living at the same time came to light in a cave at La Fère-en-Tardenois, and these belong to the Tardenoisian Culture. The Tardenoisians cut very tiny flints,

some only half an inch long, in exact shapes. Such microliths may have been attached to shafts to make darts, arrows or spears, so that small animals and birds could be killed. The wooden parts have, of course, rotted away. Microlithmakers evidently camped in summer on grassy uplands and in sandy places, for it is in such places that many of these tiny weapons have been found.

In Denmark, a race of people made axheads and picks large enough to cut down trees. They made great use of bones and antlers in making their tools, and some of them have been discovered in peaty bogs. The people who made them are called Maglemosians, a word which comes from Maglemose, meaning Great Bog. The Maglemosian Culture spread all over north Europe and to Britain, which was then joined to the mainland of Europe by marshy land.

The period during which all these tribes were living is called the Mesolithic Age, or Middle Stone Age, and it lasted for several thousand years. We know from examining the rubbish dumps of Mesolithic people that they were great fishermen as well as hunters of animals. Many of their rubbish dumps, called Kitchen Middens, have been found in Denmark, some of them 100 yards long and 50 yards wide. They have contained great

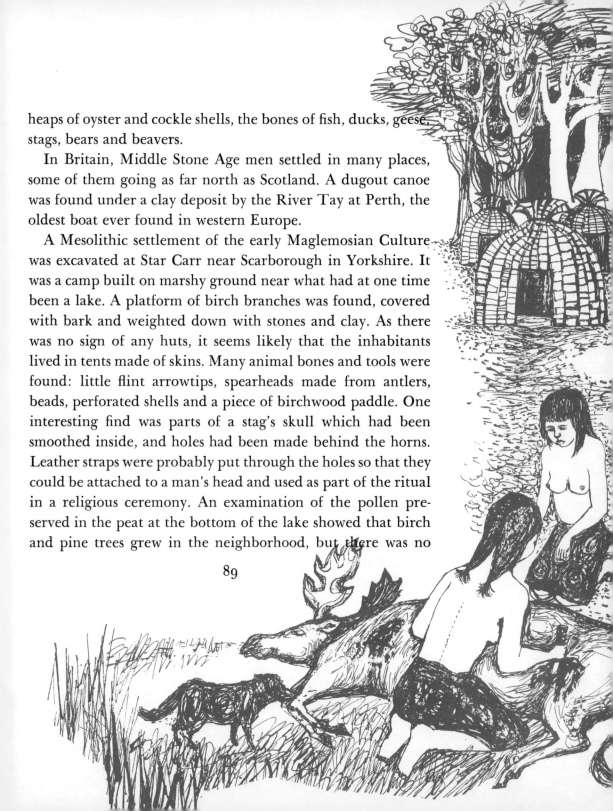

heaps of oyster and cockle shells, the bones of fish, ducks, geese, stags, bears and beavers.

In Britain, Middle Stone Age men settled in many places, some of them going as far north as Scotland. A dugout canoe was found under a clay deposit by the River Tay at Perth, the oldest boat ever found in western Europe.

A Mesolithic settlement of the early Maglemosian Culture was excavated at Star Carr near Scarborough in Yorkshire. It was a camp built on marshy ground near what had at one time been a lake. A platform of birch branches was found, covered with bark and weighted down with stones and clay. As there was no sign of any huts, it seems likely that the inhabitants lived in tents made of skins. Many animal bones and tools were found: little flint arrowtips, spearheads made from antlers, beads, perforated shells and a piece of birchwood paddle. One interesting find was parts of a stag's skull which had been smoothed inside, and holes had been made behind the horns. Leather straps were probably put through the holes so that they could be attached to a man's head and used as part of the ritual in a religious ceremony. An examination of the pollen preserved in the peat at the bottom of the lake showed that birch and pine trees grew in the neighborhood, but there was no

89

trace of hazel trees, which require a warmer climate. The settlement can therefore be dated between 7,000 and 8,000 years ago.

Bows and arrows were the chief weapons in the Middle Stone Age, and the dog became man's hunting ally. Men paddled themselves in canoes made from tree trunks which had been hollowed by fire and the use of tools. They settled in river valleys, low plains and forest clearings, and made themselves tents and huts. They fitted themselves very successfully to the changed conditions of the world, and their numbers gradually increased.

With the Neolithic Age, or New Stone Age, progress toward civilization slowly continued. It is important to remember that from now on the state of that progress varied a great deal in different parts of the world. For example, the New Stone Age began before 7000 B.C. in the Middle East, but it was not until about 2500 B.C. that it reached Britain. Wheat and barley grew wild in what is now Palestine, Syria and Iraq; rice and millet in Southeast Asia. At first it was just gathered and eaten; then it was discovered that if the seeds were set, hoed and weeded, there would be a much larger amount growing some months later, and it could be stored for times when other food was scarce. This was the beginning of agriculture. The change from hunting to farming was a major revolution in the way of life of the people. As the population increased it was possible to plant more seeds, till more of the land, and breed more animals. Gradually the wild ancestors of the dog, goat, sheep, cow and pig were domesticated and kept as flocks and herds. Families joined together to produce more food and to defend their farms. There was more time for craftsmen to make tools and decorate pots, weave cloth and build houses. They could stay in one place for a longer time, only moving on when the land became exhausted. This was a great advantage, especially if they could settle where the soil was rich and the rainfall adequate, or where a river irrigated the land. They built themselves huts and storehouses, and fortified their villages against wild animals. They found time to experiment with new ideas and gather possessions which they had never been able to have before. Even on poorer land, they could stay in one place for a whole summer and learn the crafts connected with animal rearing.

The Neolithic revolution gradually spread outward from Egypt and the Middle East, through the countries bordering the Mediterranean Sea, and up the valley of the River Danube. By 4000 B.C. it had reached Germany, Switzerland by 3000 B.C. and Britain by about 2500 B.C.

Neolithic settlements have yielded hoes, sickles and scythes made of flint. A sickle is a form of knife used for cutting grain

crops; a scythe is longer, both in the handle and the blade. Both were first made by cave dwellers in Mount Carmel in Palestine between 10,000 and 5000 B.C. The sickle was made by inserting a row of sharp flints along the edge of a curved bone. A flint sickle of this kind was found in an Egyptian granary pit. Such pits, lined with basketwork, were storage places for grain when it was harvested. When the time came for grinding it into flour, a saddle quern — a primitive hand mill — was used. The early device for grinding corn by hand consisted of two stones, the upper one moving on the lower. The lower stone was shaped like a saddle on which the upper stone was pushed backward and forward with both hands.

New Stone Age people could make baskets, spin fibers into thread, and weave the thread into fabrics. Their pots were thick and coarse. Bowls had rounded bases and were decorated with markings made either with tools or scratched on with a fingernail. The women made the pots, and they were also responsible for spinning and weaving and for the cultivation of corn.

Surprising discoveries made in Switzerland in 1854 throw light on the way some of the Neolithic communities lived. Because of a drought, the level of Lake Zurich fell considerably and the villagers of Ober-Meilen decided to take the opportunity to reclaim some of the land. While digging, they found rows of posts sticking out from the lake bed. These proved to be the piles on which Neolithic people had built their houses. Further excavations showed the timber work of the lower part of the house, pieces of woven cloth, baskets, wooden tools, horn and bone implements, fish nets, and even apples and other fruit preserved in the wet peat. It is fascinating to visualize these lake dwellings, which were joined to the mainland by a footbridge. In times of danger a section of the footbridge was removed so that the village was completely cut off from possible attack. As time went on, more lake dwellings were found in other parts of Europe, and among the relics were scraps of the earliest cloth found in western Europe, linen which was woven about 2000 B.C.

To reach Britain, Neolithic people had to cross to the sea, for Britain was by then an island. They were the first people to make huge earthworks on the tops of hills. We call such buildings causewayed camps, and there are several in southern England. One of the most famous is Windmill Hill, near Avebury in Wiltshire. It consists of several rings of high banks of earth, one inside the other, with wide ditches in between and a large space in the center. The ditches are not continuous but are in short lengths divided by entrances through which cattle could be driven. Few traces of any wooden buildings have been found in these camps, which were probably used as places of safety for cattle or for the autumn killing and hide-scraping.

At Skara Brae, in the Orkneys, a late Neolithic village was

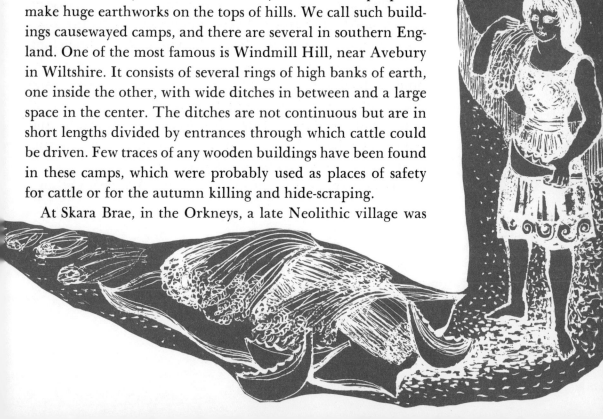

found which had been buried by drifting sand for thousands of years. The ground around the village was too poor for cultivation, so cattle- and sheep-rearing was carried on instead, together with a good deal of fishing. Six one-room cottages were uncovered, built of stone. They were very close to one another, no doubt for protection and shelter from gales, with roofed-over narrow passages between them. There was a hearth in the center of the main room of each cottage, beds were made of stone slabs, there were shelves let into the walls, and small rooms, probably storehouses, led off the main ones.

Neolithic men were miners. They did not dig for metals, which were unknown, but for flints, and the best flints were often deep underground. Several flint mines have been discovered in northern Europe. These mines have shafts up to 50 feet deep going down into the earth, with galleries branching out at the bottom along the seams of flint. The miners used the shoulder blades of cattle for shovels, and wicker baskets and ropes to haul the rubble and flint to the surface. They worked by the light given from chalk bowls filled with animal fat and wicks. The mined flint was traded with other Neolithic settlements, some of them a long way away.

Striking monuments left by New Stone Age men are long

94

barrows, found in many parts of Europe, the chalk downs of southern England, Yorkshire, Lincolnshire, Wales, Scotland and Ireland. A long barrow was a burial place for chiefs and their families. It looks like a long, grass-covered mound, higher at one end than the other. One at West Kennet in Wiltshire is nearly 400 feet long and 70 feet wide. Underneath these mounds there are passages and chambers that contain the bodies of those buried there. Ordinary people were buried without fuss in ditches or mine shafts.

There are two kinds of chambered tombs. In gallery graves, which are usually under piles of stones called cairns, the entrance opens immediately into a rectangular chamber. In passage graves, under circular cairns, there are two distinct features, a burial chamber and a passage leading to it. They belong to the late Neolithic Age and are generally found under circular barrows.

Sometimes the earth mound covering a barrow has worn away and the stones forming part of the burial chamber have become exposed. These are called Dolmens, a word which comes from two Breton words, *Dol*, a table, and *Men*, a stone. Dolmens consist of a huge single slab, the table stone, supported by two upright stones. Waylands Smithy, in Wiltshire,

W. CHAMBER

S.W. CHAMBER N.W. CHAMBER

BLOCKING STONES

S.E. CHAMBER N.E. CHAMBER

95

and Kits Coty House, in Kent, are two well-known examples. *Menhir* is another word from Brittany and means Long Stone. It is used to describe standing stones found in many countries, sometimes alone, sometimes in groups or circles. One of the largest, near Carnac in south Brittany, is more than 67 feet high. Sometimes menhirs were arranged in rows to form an avenue. At Carnac, more than a thousand stones still stand in eleven rows.

Megalith means Great Stone, and there are examples in Mediterranean countries, the west of Europe and Scandinavia. Some form part of a chambered tomb. Others, like menhirs, stand alone or in circles. In Brittany and Ireland, some of the megaliths have strange patterns carved on them — upright or wavy lines, spirals or circles, which may have been connected with magical or religious ceremonies.

There are no tombs or cemeteries in the Middle East which can be compared with those of Europe. There, Neolithic people buried their dead beneath the floors of their houses, sometimes with the heads detached from the bodies and buried separately.

The Neolithic Age not only brought great changes in the day

96

by day life of the people but also in their ways of thinking, and it saw the early stages of law and religion. When people were living in more settled communities, they needed rules and customs. Their dead stayed very close to them, and a dead chieftain was always present in their memory, so that in time he became the tribal god. In former times, magic had been used to bring success in hunting, but now that agriculture provided their food, magic was used to ensure good harvests and fat herds. Because of this, it seems that Neolithic religion was centered on the earth and the earth goddess was worshiped. People also saw a connection between their crops and the seasons, and they decided that certain things must be done at certain times so that the crops would flourish. They looked on the forces of nature as spirits, and thought that magic would bring them favors from the gods. It is possible that megaliths contained the gods of their ancestors; and stone circles may have been connected with the rotation of the sun or the cycle of the seasons. Whatever the reason for their presence, the building of these huge pillars and slabs needed great skill and strength. It is little wonder that, before the days of archaeologists, people thought them the work of giants.

97

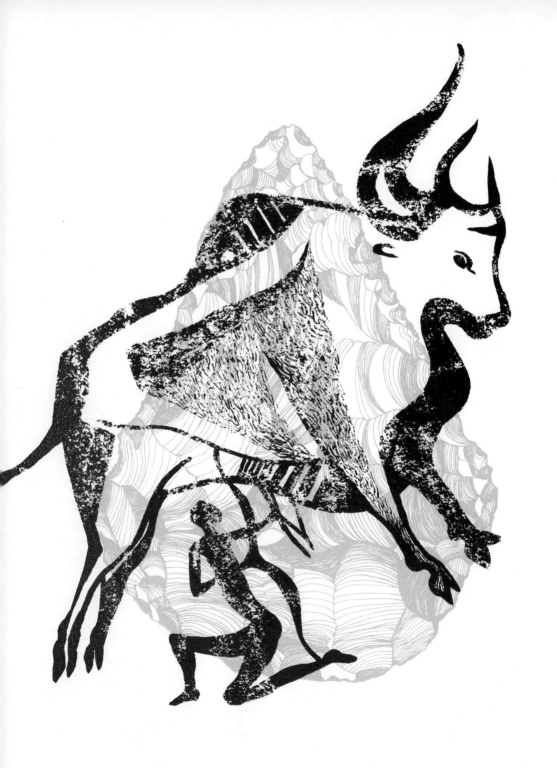

Chapter Nine

EARLY MAN IN AMERICA

UNTIL 1926, THE presence of man in America was thought to date from only a few thousand years ago. In that year, however, some artifacts were found near Folsom, New Mexico, together with the bones of extinct bison that were thought to be about 10,000 years old. Since 1926, more evidence has come to light which supports that theory, and we now believe that men were living in America even 20,000 or more years ago. The Carbon 14 date of a charred mammoth bone discovered on Santa Rosa Island, southwest of Santa Barbara, California, shows that it is possible that there were men there as far back as 30,000 years ago.

No skeletons or parts of skeletons earlier than those of Homo sapiens have been found so far. The ancestors of the American Indian probably came from the eastern half of the world. They may have moved from Asia to America by way of the Bering Strait at the end of the last Ice Age. The narrowest distance between the two continents is 56 miles, and even now it is possible to walk across it in winter. In the distant past, Asia and America were joined by a land bridge. The features of Indians have many things in common with those of Asian peoples, and this strengthens the theory of where the first Americans came from.

It is probable that there was more than one wave of migration in those long-ago times. The wanderers into the New World were skilled flintmakers and bison-hunters, and they

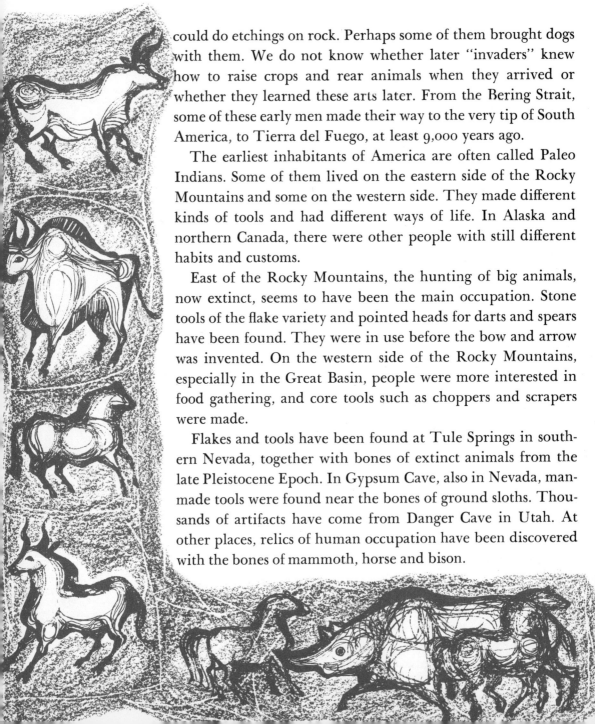

could do etchings on rock. Perhaps some of them brought dogs with them. We do not know whether later "invaders" knew how to raise crops and rear animals when they arrived or whether they learned these arts later. From the Bering Strait, some of these early men made their way to the very tip of South America, to Tierra del Fuego, at least 9,000 years ago.

The earliest inhabitants of America are often called Paleo Indians. Some of them lived on the eastern side of the Rocky Mountains and some on the western side. They made different kinds of tools and had different ways of life. In Alaska and northern Canada, there were other people with still different habits and customs.

East of the Rocky Mountains, the hunting of big animals, now extinct, seems to have been the main occupation. Stone tools of the flake variety and pointed heads for darts and spears have been found. They were in use before the bow and arrow was invented. On the western side of the Rocky Mountains, especially in the Great Basin, people were more interested in food gathering, and core tools such as choppers and scrapers were made.

Flakes and tools have been found at Tule Springs in southern Nevada, together with bones of extinct animals from the late Pleistocene Epoch. In Gypsum Cave, also in Nevada, man-made tools were found near the bones of ground sloths. Thousands of artifacts have come from Danger Cave in Utah. At other places, relics of human occupation have been discovered with the bones of mammoth, horse and bison.

The American Northwest was occupied at least 10,000 years ago by people who lived by hunting and fishing. Some of them used Burins — chisels made of flint — for working on elk antlers. Several kinds of tools have been found on the fossil beaches of Southern California.

In Alaska and northern Canada, the most famous site of early man is on the west side of Cape Denbigh in Norton Sound. Core tools, blades and burins found there resemble those of the Upper Paleolithic and Mesolithic ages in the Eastern Hemisphere.

Evidence of early man has also been found in Tamaulipas, Mexico. And in the Valley of Mexico, there are three sites where artifacts have been buried in the same levels as those containing mammoth bones. In a cave on the north shore of the Strait of Magellan, in Patagonia, stone and bone tools have been found with the bones of sloth, horse and guanaco, a member of the camel family.

It is difficult to imagine what these first Americans looked like. There are no skulls that definitely can be said to have belonged to them. The most likely specimen of early man was found near Midland, Texas. It is a longheaded skull attached to part of a skeleton and may be 12,000 years old. Scientists do not agree about two other skulls, one found near Pelican Rapids, Minnesota, and the other in the Valley of Mexico, so right now they cannot be considered genuine specimens of the first Americans. There is always hope that future discoveries will answer our questions.

Chapter Ten

THE BRONZE AGE

ABOUT 3500 B.C., men living in the Middle East discovered metals and gradually gave up flint in favor of copper and bronze, though stone tools also survived for a long time. The Bronze Age did not begin on a particular date. People did not throw away their flint implements one day and arm themselves with metal ones the next! The changeover was very slow and happened in different parts of the world at different times.

Before the use of bronze, there was a short period, lasting only a few hundred years, when copper was used — but in its raw state, not smelted. This era is usually called the Chalcolithic Age, from two Greek words, *Chalkos*, meaning copper, and *Lithos*, stone. The raw copper was merely beaten into a required shape, but the results were not always satisfactory. Copper axes were too soft to cut hardwood, and copper daggers had to be resharpened frequently. The smelting of copper nuggets reached Europe from the countries around the Aegean Sea, and they in their turn had learned the art from Anatolia and the Near East. The Egyptians used copper early in their history, and so did the people of Mesopotamia.

Silver and gold appeared almost as early as did copper. Both

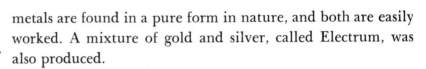

metals are found in a pure form in nature, and both are easily worked. A mixture of gold and silver, called Electrum, was also produced.

Bronze is also an alloy — a mixture of copper and tin — and is harder than copper alone. No one knows how the discovery that copper and tin could be combined was first made, but it was probably by accident. Perhaps a smith saw streaks of melting copper and tin in the stones with which his oven was built, and noticed that when they ran down to the ground and flowed together in little streams they became, when cool and hard, a tough, durable and rustless metal. Perhaps, too, as an experiment, the smith pressed a stone axhead into the ground and watched the molten alloy flow into the depression the tool had made. (It may even have been his little son who was playing near the furnace who began it all!) The result of the experiment was a perfect replica of the axhead — in bronze. From there it was a short step to putting copper and tin ores into the furnace with the deliberate intention of producing an alloy. The molten ore could then be molded into whatever shape was wanted and hammered before it hardened completely.

This new method of metalworking meant that new types of

104

weapons could be developed. Long swords grew out of chipped stone daggers. Later, in the Bronze Age, there were broad-bladed swords with double edges for two-way hacking. The polished stone ax of Neolithic times became a slim battleax, and bronze spearheads replaced those of flint.

People's lives were affected in many ways by the discovery of bronze — in time it changed the world completely. First we must go to the places where it all started and examine the conditions there before following the course of the revolution as it spread westward. The chief centers of change were in Mesopotamia, in the fertile valley between the Tigris and Euphrates rivers, where the civilizations of Sumer and Babylon arose; the Nile Valley in Egypt; the Indus Valley in India; and along the banks of the Yellow River in China. But we have much less evidence and fewer facts about what happened in India and China, so we will concentrate on Mesopotamia and Egypt, where we can trace things from the beginning.

Although the people of Neolithic times were far ahead of their Paleolithic ancestors in their attempt to live a more settled and comfortable life, they did not particularly enjoy easy times. The struggle for existence was still hard, because very

105

often the land they worked became poor and sterile and they had to move on, find new land, and start all over again. The fortunate ones were those who lived where the soil was always rich and where the climate enabled them to work in the open most of the year. The alluvial plain through which the Tigris and Euphrates ran, and the Nile delta in Egypt, were two such places where both soil and climate were favorable for agriculture and gave men leisure to think about other things and opportunity to experiment and invent. So they improved the quality and quantity of their crops by finding better methods of cultivation. Seagoing boats capable of carrying passengers took the place of dugout canoes, and sails were used for the first time.

In the Bronze Age, everything seemed to grow and spread. The population increased when families and tribes became settled. Houses were permanent structures, built to last, and in the more advanced centers of civilization, great stone palaces, temples and tombs heaved themselves into the sky. Villages became towns with paved streets and public buildings.

Trading with other towns became an important feature of

106

life, and some men grew richer than others, either because they were cleverer or more cunning. Naturally, the poorer ones were left with the hardest jobs. The former simple village headman found himself with greater power. At first he would have a council of the older and wiser men of the town to help him, but even at the beginning of the Bronze Age, the idea of kingship was beginning to appear and the rule of one man replaced the work of a group.

In Mesopotamia, each city formed a small state jealous of its independence, but in Egypt, the whole of the Nile Valley was united under one king. The king, whether of city-state or country, was all-powerful, even godlike. He owned everything, and only when he and his family were satisfied could other people share in the wealth and goods that the workers produced. In return, the king provided his subjects with certain benefits. He organized trade, planned against crop failure or famine, kept the irrigation ditches in repair, and raised an army to protect his people from invasion. Laws and religion combined to keep the king on his throne and the rest of the people in their lowly places. Gradually there grew up a sharply

defined class structure with the king and the priests at the top, merchants in the middle, and the peasants, little better than slaves, definitely at the bottom.

During the Bronze Age the ox-drawn plow was introduced, and this meant that more land could be cultivated by one family in a year. The wheel was invented, and this was as great a spur to progress as almost anything that had happened before or would happen in the future. At first it was used by the potter, and its effect was to change the crude, handmade, easily breakable pots to those of a thicker, smoother, harder, more lasting type. Later the wheel was added to carts and chariots and increased the effectiveness of both farming and warfare. It was an added inducement for men to go to war against a neighboring clan when they had chariots drawn by swift horses that could take defenders by surprise, and they were no doubt very useful, too, when it became necessary to retreat hurriedly!

The great variety of Bronze Age weapons, and the number of places where they have been found, indicate that life in those times was becoming much more warlike. Villages had to be turned into fortified camps, and methods of defense had to change to keep pace with the new weapons designed to kill (this is not unknown today), so that shields, helmets and breastplates of bronze were made to counteract the newer daggers and swords. We must remember, though, that it was only the chiefs and their warriors who would wear bronze armor. Ordinary men were no better equipped in warfare than they were in everyday life, or indeed little better than their Neolithic ancestors.

The search for copper and tin meant that travelers had to go far from their own countries, and trade became international. There was a steady stream of human traffic up and down the valleys of all the large rivers of the Near East, Europe and Russia. Such movements of people from one country to another could not help but bring about the interchange of ideas, as well as goods. Merchants learned new methods from the territories they visited and taught their hosts what was new to them. They talked to each other about their gods and told each other their legends, and every new contact made the world seem less vast and unfriendly.

In both Egypt and Mesopotamia, metals and good timber were scarce and had to be imported. It was not the raw ore that was imported, however, but the manufactured articles. The ore was smelted in the lands where it was mined, and the workmen were paid in goods that the travelers had taken with them. To do this, each state or city had to produce more goods than were needed for the people's use. When that happened society was no longer self-sufficient. The Neolithic communities could live as tight little units; those in the Bronze Age could not. They were forced to look outward beyond themselves and their own boundaries. Gradually, with the spread of goods and ideas, places such as Palestine and Syria, Persia and Anatolia, caught up with the earlier civilizations of the river valleys.

The valley of the River Danube acted as a natural trade route, and southern Russia and the eastern Ukraine came under the influence of the Bronze Age. Then the wandering traders moved west into central Europe, and during the last 2000 years B.C., the knowledge of smelting ores and manufacturing the "new" weapons and tools, was widely spread throughout Europe.

Two of the most important metal deposits were the copper ore of Hungary and the tin ore of Bohemia. A large hoard of bronze implements has been found in a village in Czechoslovakia called Aunjetitz. Tin or copper were also found in Italy, northwest Spain, Brittany, and Cornwall in Britain. And wherever the making of bronze was introduced, other fashions changed. Pottery of a high standard was made, good buildings with painted designs on the walls were put up, and although megalithic monuments continued to be built in the north and west of Europe, burial in a barrow (a circular earthbuilt mound or tumulus) became common, and later in the Bronze Age, the ashes rather than the bodies of the dead were put in the burial chamber in cinerary urns.

The Bronze Age reached Britain about 1900 B.C., brought by men who originally came from the eastern side of the Mediterranean. Though they brought bronze weapons with them, they were probably not metalworkers themselves. We call them the Beaker Folk from the shape of the pots they made, which were buried with their dead.

Stonehenge, the great circle of standing stones in the English county of Wiltshire, is one of the most remarkable and impressive monuments of the Bronze Age. Although it was started by Neolithic people, the Beaker Folk had most to do with it. When complete, it consisted of a circular earthen mound, inside which were two circles of stones. The outer circle had 30 large, upright stones connected by flat stones resting across the tops; the inner circle was made of smaller stones. Inside this, there were 2 horseshoe shapes, one of 5 trilithons (a group of 3 stones, 2 of them upright and a third lying across them). The other horseshoe was of smaller stones standing alone. An avenue of two earthen banks led away from the monument.

Stonehenge was probably used as a temple, a meetingplace, and for ceremonial gatherings, but there are mysteries about it that archaeologists have never solved. Some of the stones were

111

brought from the Prescelly Mountains in Wales, 150 miles away, and one of the mysteries is how the builders managed to transport 80 of these massive stones such a great distance. The most probable theory is that they were carried over water and land on rafts, along the coast, up the Bristol Channel and along the Avon and Frome rivers — a route that would mean more water than land travel. The task must have taken many men a very long time; the raising of the stones, too, must have been very difficult. It has been calculated that 200 men would have been needed to erect a single stone of the outer circle.

Avebury, also in Wiltshire, was another Beaker Folk building, earlier and even larger than Stonehenge. It is the largest known megalithic circle and was probably used as a sacred enclosure. A bank and a ditch formed a circle enclosing an area of nearly 30 acres, but many of the stones that once formed two circles inside the outer one have disappeared. Some were destroyed in the Middle Ages, and some were broken up in the seventeenth century, in order to build cottages. Near Avebury, at Silbury Hill, is the largest artificial hill in Europe. It covers 5½ acres, is in the shape of a pyramid, and is 125 feet high. It has not been fully excavated, so that who built it and when are further mysteries. Its size suggests that it was the barrow of a very important person — perhaps even the chief who was responsible for the Avebury monument.

When other people from northern Europe reached Britain about 1500 B.C. and took the place of the Beaker Folk, they already knew how to make weapons, tools and ornaments of bronze. The new invaders were great traders. They brought gold from Ireland, amber from the Baltic countries, and beads from Crete and Egypt. About this time the third stage of Stonehenge was built. Their warriors wore the kind of helmets, breastplates and shields that had been in use in eastern Europe hundreds of years before, and the women wore earrings and necklaces of gold and jet beads. Both men and women wore twisted ribbons made of gold, called Torcs, around their necks.

Between 1500 and 750 B.C. other tribes appeared in Britain, each becoming prominent in its turn, and then came the Celts from central and western Europe, bringing with them a new form of plow. It had no wheels but was light and could be drawn by two oxen. Village farming became the normal way

115

of life. For the first time, horses were used to draw carts. Weapons were sharper and more elaborate, and in their jewelry the Celts used electrum and an alloy of gold and copper, as well as bronze.

Thus the discoveries made by more advanced people living in the Mediterranean countries came across the Channel to Britain, one of the last European outposts of the Neolithic Age. And when Britain was in the throes of its bronze revolution, the Middle East had progressed still more and was enjoying the benefits that the use of iron brought.

Civilization in the Bronze Age mainly depended on three things: the charcoal-fed furnace (replacing the wood-burning open hearth of Neolithic times), which not only changed the art of pottery but meant the easier smelting of the ores and the manufacture of the articles that were making life so different; the wheel, first used by the potter and then as an aid to the farmer and the soldier; and — writing.

Writing has not been mentioned so far, even though it was invented in the Middle East during the Bronze Age, because, strictly speaking, it has nothing to do with the quest for prehistory. When men began to write, real history began. Writing is part of civilization, part of the life of the cities that grew up

116

during these times. When trade became important, it was necessary to record what was bought and sold. Stores had to be counted, lists of what belonged to the king made out, and accounts drawn up. Writing was invented in Sumer and in Egypt, though the Phoenicians were the first people to use a real alphabet sometime before 1500 B.C. They passed on to the Greeks, from whom the Romans adopted it, and then the people of western Europe. Eastward, the alphabet was taken to Mesopotamia, Iran, and eventually to India.

Writing first took the form of Pictograms, in which a picture represented an object. Then Ideograms, in which it represented an idea, were introduced, and thirdly, Phonograms, in which it stood for an actual spoken sound. In Egypt, the pictographic form is called Hieroglyphic, and in Mesopotamia, Cuneiform. The story of writing, however — like the story of the Iron Age — does not come within the scope of this book. When archaeologists can read the history of a tribe or nation on the tablets, cylinders and monuments which the people themselves inscribed, then they are not dealing with prehistory. Although in Britain, prehistory lasted until the coming of the Romans in A.D. 43, in the east it ended many hundreds of years earlier.

117

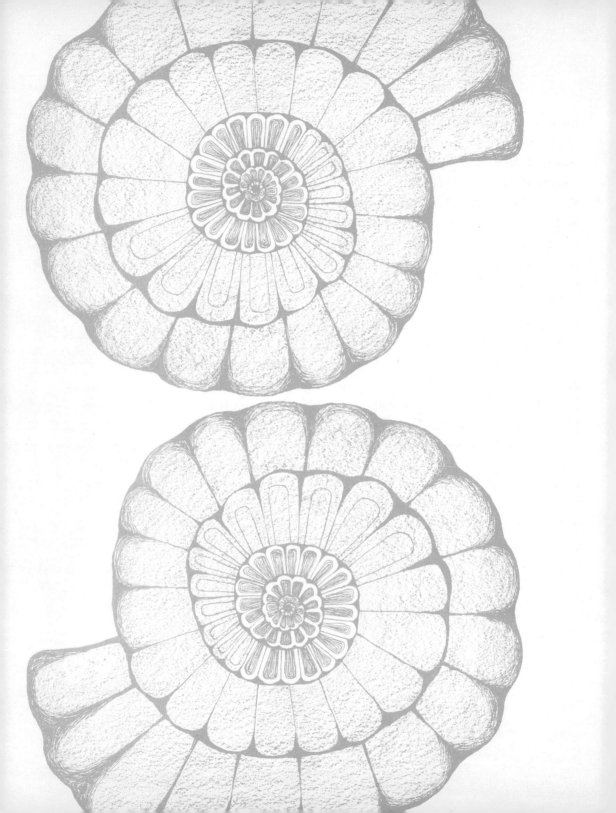

In general we may say that the Bronze Age forms the bridge by which we leave prehistory. It is the link by which the times we live in are tied to the past that was once forgotten but that is now gradually being revealed by the patient work of the archaeologist.

From the beginning of the world to the end of the Bronze Age, more than 4,000 million years slid by. In a short guide to prehistory it is not possible to do more than glide over this vast period of time, pausing here and there, but having to leave huge gaps and lump together thousands and millions of years at a time, and skimming over the changes that have taken place — from the first stirrings of life in water to the appearance of human beings, from the first stone toolmakers to the skilled workers in metal.

119

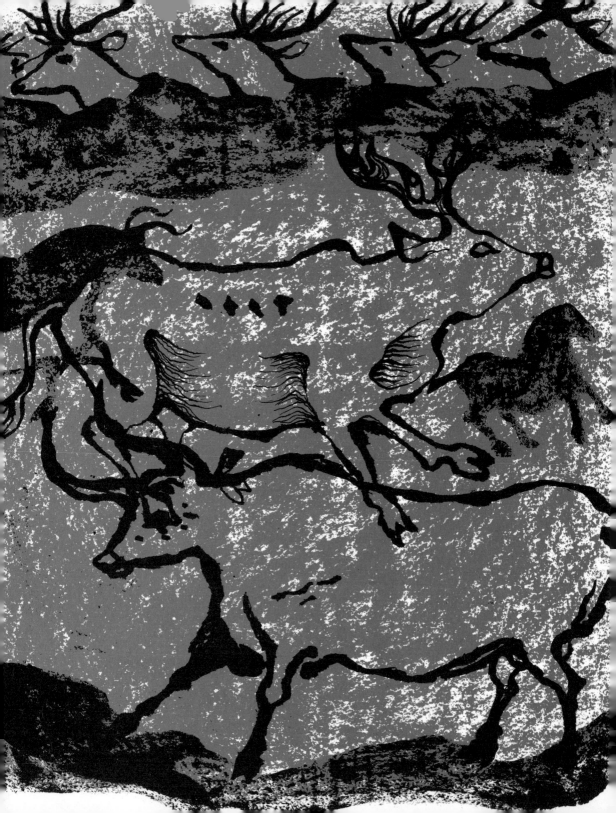

The plot of the greatest mystery story of all time has been laid bare, but bare bones need flesh to cover them, and the "flesh" of prehistory can be found by further reading, by visiting museums, and by actually becoming an archaeologist. There are many books about every aspect of the prehistoric past, and in them you can read in much greater detail about dinosaurs, Old Stone Age people, or life in Bronze Age Sumer. In museums you can see the skulls, pottery, coins, jewelry and weapons you have read about. On the seashore, in the country, in quarries and on cliffs, you will have the chance of finding for yourselves — as so many boys and girls have done — the fascinating clues that help to make the puzzle of the past clearer. There are many secrets still hidden in the earth — hardly a month passes without a fresh discovery being made — but many questions about early men remain unanswered. The future holds exciting possibilities. The quest for prehistory will never be finished.

BIBLIOGRAPHY

Atkinson, R. C. J., *Stonehenge*. Penguin, 1962.

Brodrick, Alan Houghton, *Man and His Ancestry*. Premier, 1964.

Carrington, Richard, *A Guide to Earth History*. Mentor.

Carrington, Richard, *A Million Years of Man*. Mentor, 1964.

Cole, Sonia, *The Neolithic Revolution*. British Museum, 1961.

Cottrell, Leonard (ed.), *Concise Encyclopedia of Archaeology*. Hawthorn Books, 1960.

Fox, Cyril, *Life and Death in the Bronze Age*. Humanities Press, 1959.

Hawkes, Jacquetta, *A Land*. Random House, 1952.

Hawkes, Jacquetta, *Man on Earth*. Random House, 1955.

Hawkes, Jacquetta and Christopher, *Prehistoric Britain*. Penguin, 1944.

Kühn, Herbert, *On the Track of Prehistoric Man*. Random House, 1955.

Mellersh, H. E. L., *The Story of Early Man*. Viking Press, 1959.

Montagu, Ashley, *Man: His First Million Years*. Signet, 1959.

Rhodes, F. H. T., *The Evolution of Life*. Penguin, 1962.

Senet, André, *Man in Search of His Ancestors*. McGraw-Hill, 1955.

Von Koenigswald, G. H. R., *Meeting Prehistoric Man*. Harper, 1957.

Winbolt, S. E., *Britain B.C.* Penguin, 1943.

INDEX

About the Authors

GEOFFREY PALMER has written several books on archaeology and folklore. He is the Headmaster of a large primary school in London, England.

NOEL LLOYD has collaborated with Mr. Palmer in books of fiction, folk tales, ghost stories, archaeology and music. His home is in London.

DATE DUE

GAYLORD

PRINTED IN U.S.A.